**PRAISE FOR *HEROES, VILLAINS, AND THE THRILL OF PROFESSIONAL SELLING* AND ADRIAN DAVIS**

Adrian is a deep friend and business partner. Here, his true depth of wisdom wrapped in narrative and metaphor is on full display. This book will fundamentally reframe your perspective and approach to how you "occupy your space" in the future of strategic selling. He has drawn on the wisdom of the ages and made it consumable for all of us to be a "special resource" in our personal and professional lives. This book is a true gift for you to unwrap and then give away as you make resulting changes to how you engage with others in life and work. Unpack, unwrap, and unleash the tools and design principles Adrian has curated and created for us all.

**—Phil Styrlund**
*CEO, the Summit Group*

*Heroes, Villains, and the Thrill of Professional Selling* is the type of book that can transform the way you interact with others. Adrian has developed a framework based on proven neuroscience concepts that is a meaningful, compelling, and enjoyable concept. Stories have nurtured our lives since our childhoods. In this book Adrian shows us how to leverage the full potential of stories through an analogy that speaks to anyone. It's a very powerful tool that can be applied even in your personal life (try it with your kids—it works!).

**—Florent Bühler**
*Digital marketing innovation director, MSD France*

Adrian uses the very relatable analogy of moviemaking to describe how salespeople can go from good to great. If you're looking for a compelling, punchy read that will challenge your assumptions about your role in sales, the role of your customers, and the companies you're targeting, you've found the right book. We all want to be heroes in our own organization. This book shows you how, if you're prepared to sidestep that role in your customers' own stories, you can achieve exactly that.

**—Catherine Grainger**
*Development and education manager, 3M*

This is a great piece of work! In this book Adrian succeeds in drawing a parallel between selling and making a movie. A must-read for understanding who the real "hero" in the sales process should be.

**—Lonnie Essex**
*VP of global accounts, AVI-SPL*

I was blown away by the innovative approach taken in this book. The use of movie analogies to illustrate key points made it not only relatable and easy to follow, but also highly memorable. As a sales leader, I found this book to be an invaluable resource for inspiring my team and helping us stay relevant to our customers. I highly recommend it to anyone looking to take their sales strategies to the next level.

**—Susan Milwit**
*Global account manager, AVI-SPL*

I'm a huge film buff, and I write about sales and marketing. If anyone had told me movie production was like sales, I would have waved them away. And then I read *Heroes, Villains, and the Thrill of Professional Selling*. In his book Adrian Davis uses stories to reveal their power in sales settings. Through movie metaphors, readers learn how the hero's story applies to sales and how to craft emotional, personal stories that guide buyers on a journey in which they emerge as the hero in their new world. (Yes, that C-suite decision maker is like Tom Hanks's role in *Captain Philip*.) More than that, though, Davis gives readers concrete strategies and methods to help salespeople write and direct their own winning buyer experiences. If you are a salesperson or manage a team of sellers, add this book to your reading list.

**—Michelle Davidson**
*Marketer and media strategist, Allego*


I absolutely love this book! The concepts and tools that Adrian shares are all so logical and easy to comprehend. Adrian takes us on a journey through the process of selling, which is truly like a movie, with a hero, characters, cast members, and a villain. As we go through this journey, Adrian tells it in such a relatable and engaging way, all the while sharing his own story, as well as tips, techniques, and tools that have helped him to be successful. I was immediately drawn in and can easily apply the concepts to any sales situation!

**—Kat McQuade**
*Director of technical training, TPL Composites, Inc.*

Adrian Davis should be locked up in chains for giving away the keys to the customer centricity castle! Davis's inspiring approach is elegant but refreshingly simple. He replaces hardwired product-focused selling—the kind of old-school sales mindset that's nearly everybody's default—with what he calls the hero's journey. As a commercial sales leader and serial lifelong learner, Adrian teaches his own special innovation that has been crafted over thirty years; it's a nonjudgmental, nonreactive way of developing key skills for account development and management through lessons of listening, storytelling, relationship building, and most importantly recognizing who the hero is in your personal movie. While most reads can feel like they are written in an ivory tower, Adrian's real-world application offers clarity and calm in the critical moments before taking decisive action as we work to close the first of many opportunities with must-win customers.

**—Paul Lazzaro**
*Director of talent management and leadership development, Otsuka*

I highly recommend *Heroes, Villains, and the Thrill of Professional Selling* for anyone looking to improve their sales skills. Adrian Davis provides valuable insights, strategies, and techniques to effectively communicate with potential customers, build lasting relationships, and close deals. The book is filled with compelling stories that are relatable and easy to understand along with practical tips and real-world examples. Whether you're a seasoned sales professional or just starting, this book is packed with valuable insights and actionable advice that will help you close more deals and boost your sales performance. It's a must-read for anyone looking to take their sales game to the next level.

**—Mark Wickware**
*SVP and NA leader, GrowthSpace*

True to his message, Adrian shares a comprehensive set of tools and proven sales methodologies by applying the book's own underlying theme—the power of storytelling. Each page feels like a personal conversation with Adrian himself, approachable, emotional, engaging. Behind every concept shared are our own real sales successes, heroic journeys, and lessons learned. Adrian brings honor and meaning to the science and art that is professional selling, and he has provided us with a book to be read and revisited as a compass for anyone with a vision, a message, or a purpose they are seeking to advance.

**—Brett Bailey**
*VP sales, WBM Technologies*

It's time to refresh your thinking and update your approach! *Heroes, Villains, and the Thrill of Professional Selling* will take you to the next level. New to your role? This book is a must-read to jump-start your career in strategic account management. Adrian Davis's creative approach with practical application includes proven methods and processes that align with today's strategic business visions, allowing you to attain your personal and professional goals.

The hero's journey is outlined perfectly and is reiterated throughout the book for continued understanding. This provides the opportunity to create and live out your own "story."

This book offers a multitude of resources to assist you throughout your sales and strategic account management journey. Utilize these resources to enhance your engagement with a capital E!

**—Debbie DeBolt**
*Senior key account manager, Bellevue University–*
*Corporate Learning Solutions*

Adrian changed my sales team's mindset and our approach to our customers. By implementing his methods, we changed our relationship with key accounts from being just another vendor to a valued strategic partner. We've also renewed numerous, very large agreements as a result. Engaging Adrian Davis is one of the best investments we've ever made.

**—Blake Jarrell**
*Director, Customer Success, TRIOSE, Inc.; Former operations manager, AmerisourceBergen*

# HEROES, VILLAINS, AND THE THRILL OF PROFESSIONAL SELLING

# HEROES, VILLAINS, AND THE THRILL OF PROFESSIONAL SELLING

Your Guide to Directing

a Winning Buying Experience

## ADRIAN DAVIS

Advantage | Books

Published by Advantage Books, Charleston, South Carolina.
An imprint of Advantage Media.

ADVANTAGE is a registered trademark, and the Advantage colophon is a trademark of Advantage Media Group, Inc.

Printed in the United States of America.

10  9  8  7  6  5  4  3  2  1

ISBN: 978-1-64225-546-1 (Paperback)
ISBN: 978-1-64225-545-4 (eBook)

LCCN: 2023906783

Cover design by Matthew Morse.
Layout design by Megan Elger.

Advantage Books is an imprint of Advantage Media Group. Advantage Media helps busy entrepreneurs, CEOs, and leaders write and publish a book to grow their business and become the authority in their field. Advantage authors comprise an exclusive community of industry professionals, idea-makers, and thought leaders. For more information go to **advantagemedia.com**.

*To my mother, who taught me the powerful, lifelong lesson of resilience when facing despair.*

# CONTENTS

# ACT III: APPLICATION

## ACKNOWLEDGMENTS

I'd like to acknowledge a few people who were of great assistance to me in writing this book.

Kathy Palakoff of GoFirestarter. Kathy, thank you so much for bringing clarity to my thinking. I appreciate the way you listened carefully and helped me to formulate my thoughts and deliver them in such a clear framework. As I've said to you many times, you're scary smart!

Phil Styrlund of the Summit Group. Phil, I'm so grateful for your visionary leadership. Thank you for all your encouragement and for being such a great sounding board and friend. The world needs more leaders like you!

Brett Bailey and JoeAnne Hardy of WBM Technologies. Thank you for giving me the honor of accompanying you on your hero's journey. You are such great leaders because you are such wonderful human beings. Thanks for being so open and transparent and trusting me at the beginning of my journey. I appreciate your commitment to execution and the opportunity I've had to see my ideas put into practice with stellar results.

# FOREWORD

**W**e can all relate to the concept of heroes and villains when we think of our sales activities. Yet I was struck by the brilliant and relatable analogy of comparing sales to movies—how good storytelling is only part of the equation when what began as an idea finds success on the silver screen or in the marketplace.

The Strategic Account Management Association (SAMA) has been around nearly sixty years, and the concept of "cocreating value" is at the center of our story, our strategy, and our successful, long-term relationships with clients. This book now describes an approach to creating that value—one that draws upon proven techniques from the movie industry and is imperative for mutual success: *your client is the hero in the story.*

Simple to say, maybe obvious to understand, and not at all natural to execute! And even though, as salespeople, we're drawn to the bottom line of box-office numbers, sales is never the hero or the focus—it's the client.

In this book Adrian Davis simplifies the hero's journey with real-life examples, compelling stories, and templates to guide you. Additionally, the book goes well beyond explaining the hero's journey and offers years of experience in client discovery and insights.

As we learn, the salesperson is the director of this story. It's their role to lead the team to create a positive buying experience. You must immerse yourself in someone else's world, but it is certainly not a "one-size-fits-all" scenario. Movie genres are an excellent and relevant way to understand different clients and environments. Are they action, complex thriller, romance, sci-fi, drama, comedy, horror? All these genres can fit, and they all have relevance to working with your client.

Adding to this insight, Adrian offers a simple methodology in storytelling, a path to develop your SOCKET solution, and a way to engage "inside-outsiders" to help in the journey. In all my years at SAMA, I find the greatest takeaways from the book to be a robust series of one hundred questions to discover value and a stakeholder checklist to guide you through the maze.

Your ability to engage, discover, and relate to your client may be dependent on your ability to know your "hero's journey" and tell the story. Take Adrian's advice and don't come out of the story to editorialize—let the story do the work! You can read his lessons learned, put them into practice, and embark on your own journey for stronger relationships and success.

**—Denise Freier**
*President and CEO, Strategic Account Management Association*

# INTRODUCTION

**M**any would say I was a troubled teenager. I guess I was. I certainly lacked focus. School was easy, but it made no sense to me. I didn't understand the "why" behind what I was being taught. This frustrated me and led me to becoming a homeless high school dropout. Long story short: while figuring out how to put my life together, I discovered the sales profession … and I loved it! It immediately made sense to me, and for the first time I found meaning in my work. I couldn't understand why sales was considered dishonorable. I set myself two goals. The first was to learn all I could to become a successful salesperson, and the second was to prove that one could be successful in sales and also honorable.

Looking back on my career now, I feel a deep sense of fulfillment. I never wavered in my objectives, and I have achieved both. This book is one way I feel like I am giving back, hopefully helping others along their journey as I have been helped by others on my journey.

This book was designed as a practical tool for busy business leaders, particularly those who are responsible for revenue-generating sales in their companies. I've added a bit of fun by using a movie analogy because, in my experience as a corporate sales trainer, learning is way more effective when it's entertaining and engaging. Moreover, let me assure you that the comparison between making sales and making movies is remarkably accurate.

First, let's talk about the name of this book—*Heroes, Villains, and the Thrill of Professional Selling: Your Guide to Directing a Winning Buying Experience.* I love sales and find it thrilling to help customers solve their problems. I believe our customers—not we—are the heroes. That attitude places customers front and center as we direct the buying experience. And we do direct it with a strategic and deliberate approach. Nothing about sales is random; it requires discipline and purpose. I also believe that there has been an uptick in external forces, or what I call "the villains," that are putting businesses in a constant state of uncertainty. Our job in professional selling is to recognize those villains and help our hero-customers thrive in the midst of what are often chaotic forces. We are accompanying them on their "hero's journey," which I'll address more as we move through the book. As professional salespeople and strategic account managers, we are the directors of their buying experience.

These beliefs make up the core of this book, which is a sequel to my previous book published ten years ago, *Human to Human Selling: How to Sell Real and Lasting Value in an Increasingly Digital and Fast-Paced World.* I emphasized "human to human" in my first book because I could see the wave of automation, e-commerce, and artificial intelligence that was encroaching on the world of professional selling. Much has changed in the last ten years, particularly with the two-year pandemic shutdown and its ongoing implications. But what has not changed is that complex and high-value B2B sales and account management is, and will always remain, a human-to-human discipline.

When I originally started writing this book, I focused primarily on storytelling, which has been a fundamental aspect of my work for more than thirty years. I quickly realized that there are lots of books, courses, and webinars on storytelling and sales. Many take the stance that delivering an engaging story to a prospect is the key to sales. The message that good storytelling equals good sales is somewhat simplistic. It's just not that basic.

Professional selling goes far beyond delivering a good story. It requires creating a winning buying experience that generates referrals and repeat business. It demands collaboration from teams on both the seller and buyer sides. It often requires significant people and financial resources. Each sales opportunity has its own plot, although the story flow may be similar depending on the type of sale and industry. These realizations led me to the belief that professional selling is more similar to moviemaking. Storytelling is an important part of the process, but it's only part of the equation.

I'll provide you with a way to look at customer types through the lens of movie genres. Does your potential customer have a culture that seems like an action movie? Are they in need of a little bit of romance? Do you need to help them

> *The message that good storytelling equals good sales is somewhat simplistic. It's just not that basic.*

escape from a horror situation? See, I told you we could have a bit of fun with this analogy, while learning key principles that will flow right to your bottom line.

Throughout this book I use the terms "professional salesperson" and "strategic account manager." This is a deliberate decision to emphasize the professional nature of sales and the critical strategic role of account managers, since both are vital in creating and sustaining a winning buying experience. While professional salespeople are clearly responsible for successfully completing transactions with customers, this is not necessarily the case for strategic account managers. In many organizations the strategic account manager never actually finalizes business transactions. They provide strategic coordination that enables the sales team to close more business. However, they are equally if not even more committed to creating compelling value for their customers.

The thousands of people I've trained have found three guides particularly useful in putting this thinking to work, and I'll be sharing these powerful documents with you:

- The Hero's Journey: Discovery Storyboard

- The Hero's Journey: Success Storyboard

- The Hero's Journey: Action Storyboard

The discovery storyboard is based on structured story listening that's part of the discovery process. Just like movie directors rely on storyboards to capture the flow and vision of a movie, sales teams can use a storyboard to understand core aspects of the engagement. I've created terminology to make the method more memorable and to emphasize key aspects of this very important process:

- The Hero

- The Goal

- The Villain

- The Flaw

- The Pit of Despair

- The Special Resource

- The New World

Next, I'll show you a proven method you can use to tell a relevant success story to a customer so that it hooks their emotions and facilitates engagement. Finally, I'll share a simple road map for once the sale is closed in order to produce a successful engagement that leads to repeat business.

Each of these three storyboards can be found online at our academy (https://academy.whetstoneinc.ca). I strongly advise that you print them off and fill in your answers by hand. There is a significant amount of research that indicates that writing on paper instead of typing on a computer slows the brain down for more thoughtful answers that are retained longer.

Finally, I will summarize lessons we can learn from Hollywood. By the end of the book, you will have a fresh outlook on sales. The latest findings from neuroscience will be accessible and practical. Not only will you be able to effectively engage your customers at a deeper emotional level, but you'll also have a lot more fun. As artificial intelligence tools like ChatGPT, Midjourney, and DALL-E 2 threaten to replace transactional selling, the simple approaches that you learn in this book will make you indispensable to your employer and your most important customers. This book is less about techniques and much more about thinking approaches. As customer relationships are increasingly disrupted by artificial intelligence, how you think and how you help your customers to think and make sense of their world will make you more valuable. The future is bright for those who understand that the more the world changes, the more customers will seek higher level partnerships that help them navigate these changes.

For more extensive tools, classes, coaching, and advisory groups, please join the Whetstone Academy at https://academy.whetstoneinc.ca. You can also contact me directly at https://whetstoneinc.ca/contact-us/ to inquire about speaking engagements and live, instructor-led training.

# ACT I: KEY CONCEPTS

# CHAPTER 1

# STORYTELLING AND MOVIEMAKING

*Storytelling is the most powerful way*
*to put ideas into the world.*
**—Robert McAfee Brown, minister, theologian, activist**

I discovered the power of storytelling accidentally. I was head-hunted by Silicon Valley–based Portal Software to represent them in Canada. This was back in the late 1990s, and the company was an early internet-based business. Its biggest competitor was headquartered in Toronto. I nearly refused the offer because I was concerned that I would be its only professional salesperson in Canada but decided not to miss the opportunity since I knew the internet was going to be big.

Within a month of joining, I was flown out to California for a sales conference where I met my peers from around the world. At that point I had no customers or success stories of my own and intuitively understood that I needed success stories, or I would fail. Failure was never, and has never been, an option for me. So, I asked my peers one question: "Where have you been successful?" As they told me their stories, I jotted a summary on blank sheets at the back of my FranklinCovey planner. By the end of the conference, I had about thirty stories to use with potential customers.

This "story library" was proof that Portal Software could deliver real value even though it was a start-up. Every time I got a lead, I would do background research in preparation for my first meeting. Then I would review my story library and decide which stories were most relevant based on factors such as industry, size, geography, potential business objectives, and challenges. After asking a set of robust discovery questions, I would weave the relevant stories into our conversations. My formula was simple:

1. Meet with senior business executives.

2. Take a genuine interest in what they were trying to accomplish.

3. Tell them a story about someone with similar goals who became successful working with us.

It worked like a charm. In fact, it worked so well that when the economy went into a recession and many of my colleagues were laid off, I continued to crush it. I carried a $6 million quota and did $18 million (300 percent of quota). What's ironic is that I used examples from former sales reps who had not taken advantage of their own success stories to help retain their jobs.

Back then I was guided by intuition. Now, after years of research, guided by books such as William Storr's *Science of Storytelling* and Lisa Cron's *Wired for Story* and decades of working with sales teams, I understand that stories reduce the friction of empathizing with others. When we tell stories, people immerse themselves and live vicariously in the story as if the plotline is happening to them. They imagine and are immersed in an alternate reality. Once they've experienced this alternate reality, they become open to this course of action if they feel it is superior to their current course. The magic of storytelling is it enables us to be provocative without coming across as arrogant, insulting, or offensive. We all know that no one wants to be told their baby is ugly, but everyone would like a prettier baby. People find it easier to consider their baby might be ugly when they hear the story of someone else who came to terms with their ugly baby and found a way to make their baby prettier. Looking back, I can see the exact moment when multi-million-dollar decisions were made and when key decision makers imagined their success through someone else's story. I don't want you to think that it came easy for me. I still had to work really hard, but I was fortunate that I had stumbled onto the process of using stories in my sales presentations. I didn't know why they worked. They just did.

Our world is all about stories. Sometimes, they are told in a book. Other times they are visual like a piece of art. Sometimes, they are stories we orally pass down from generation to generation. Other times, they come in the form of a song lyric.

In recent years experts have theorized about how stories impact our brains. In their book *Made to Stick*, best-selling authors Chip and Dan Heath provide some insight: "When we read books, we have the sensation of being drawn into the author's world. When friends tell us stories, we instinctively empathize. When we watch movies, we identify with the protagonists." They go on to say, "One team of researchers has produced some exciting evidence suggesting that the line between a story's 'audience' and a story's 'protagonist' may be a bit blurry."[1]

What do they mean by "a bit blurry"? In many ways we begin to feel the way the protagonist does in the story. We begin to see through their eyes and can relate that view to our own world. The

---

1    Chip Heath and Dan Heath, *Made to Stick* (New York: Penguin Random House, 2007).

Heaths continue, "These studies suggest that there's no such thing as a passive audience. When we hear a story, our minds move from room to room. When we hear a story, we simulate it." Think of the many times you've watched a movie and felt your heart begin to race as the protagonist is in imminent danger. That's an example of the simulation the Heaths are talking about.

Simulate can mean visualization. At a fundamental level, our brains think in pictures. When we hear a story, our mind's eye creates a picture that goes with the story. It's almost as if a movie is running in our heads. What's the point of visualization? According to the Heaths, "Mental simulation is not as good as actually doing something, but it's the next best thing. And, to circle back to the world of sticky ideas, what we're suggesting is that the right kind of story is, effectively, a simulation. Stories are like flight simulators for the brain."

When we share a success story with a potential customer, they feel what the customer from our previous engagement felt and experienced. That's the power of story. That's why stories are so impactful when used correctly during sales presentations. Stories open the door to the mind of your customer. More importantly, stories open their heart. Humans long to connect with other humans, and we long to feel deeply for and about others.

As I began thinking about the connections between movies and professional sales, I thought of movies that stand out in my mind. You can see from the following list that they cross over multiple genres. Yet, despite their differences, they share commonalities that are interesting to me and, more importantly, reflect some key aspects of professional selling. As you're reading this book, I suggest that you make your own list of movie favorites (and maybe check out a couple of mine if you haven't seen them). I think you will find composing your own list a revealing exercise into your personality and sales techniques. Here is my list:

- *Braveheart*
- *Captain Fantastic*
- *Captain Phillips*
- *Chicken Run*
- *Forrest Gump*
- *Harriet*
- *Marriage Story*
- *Parasite*
- *The Invisible Guest*
- *The Pianist*
- *White Tiger*

What's yours?

In the space below, make a list of some of your favorite movies. As you learn more about story structure, go back and watch some of these movies and see if you can deconstruct why they were so engaging for you.

| # | MOVIE TITLE |
|---|---|
| 1 | |
| 2 | |
| 3 | |
| 4 | |
| 5 | |
| 6 | |
| 7 | |
| 8 | |
| 9 | |
| 10 | |

# Comparing Professional Sales to Movies

Professional sales, like movies, follow a storyline. There's the beginning where we get to know the characters, and a problem is articulated. Someone is killed. A romance breaks up. A planet is invaded. The gang goes on a badly planned road trip. The problems are endless and varied, just like in a company. A new competitor enters the market. Sales are on a downward turn. Economic lockdowns disrupt the supply chain.

Next is the middle where there are lots of plot twists and complexities. In professional sales it can be things like changes in the customer's requirements, leadership upheaval, or market conditions. Finally, there's the conclusion where the story is resolved. Maybe it's a happily-ever-after ending. Maybe it's a lesson learned. And hopefully there's even room for a sequel or the next engagement with the customer.

Professional sales, like movies, have a hero. We need to emotionally identify with the hero to be engaged in the story. And here's a very important caveat. *The hero is never the salesperson. The hero is always the customer.* Too often salespeople place themselves in the hero role. This attitude negatively impacts customer relationships. This is so important, I'd better repeat it. *The hero is never the salesperson. The hero is always the customer.*

Your customer is engaged in a hero's journey. This term was popularized by Joseph Campbell, an American writer and literature professor whose focus was comparative mythology and religion.

Regarding Campbell's hero's journey, CBC Radio, in a 2019 article, stated, "Hidden inside the plots of blockbuster movies like *The Matrix*

> *The hero is never the salesperson. The hero is always the customer.*

**17**

and *The Lion King* is a storytelling structure called the 'hero's journey.' That structure found its biggest success in the 1977 megahit, *Star Wars*, which was directly inspired by it."[2]

In Campbell's best-known book from 1949, *The Hero with a Thousand Faces*, he puts forth his theory about the twelve stages of the archetypal hero's journey shared by world mythologies.

*The traditional twelve stages of the hero's journey.*

I have simplified the twelve stages of the hero's journey to six simple steps as it relates to professional sales and strategic account management:

---

2    CBC Radio, "How Mythologist Joseph Campbell Made Luke Skywalker a Hero," September 3, 2019, https://www.cbc.ca/radio/ideas/how-mythologist-joseph-campbell-made-luke-skywalker-a-hero-1.5262649.

# The Hero's Journey

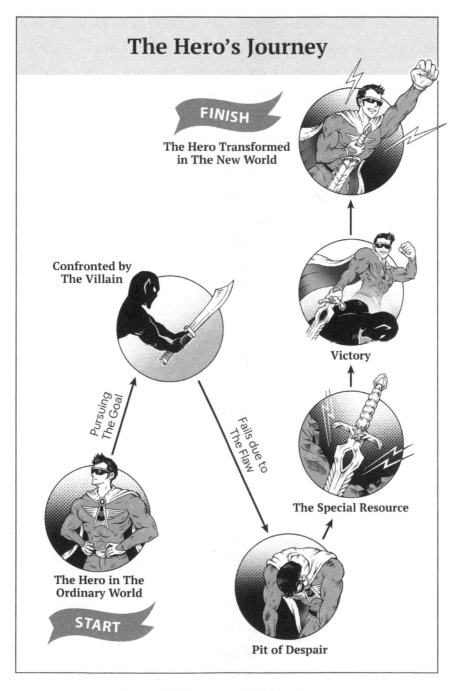

The simplified six stages of the hero's journey.

While Joseph Campbell popularized this framework for modern storytelling, it is an ancient framework. Campbell, himself, acknowledged that it is a fundamental, universal narrative pattern that can be found in the myths and stories of all cultures. Essentially, when applied to sales, it is the storyline that takes us through the customer's experience: understanding goals, examining external and internal forces that are preventing them from achieving their goals, finding and implementing a solution, and the customer's transformation into a new way of doing things. As this is an ancient, universal framework that reflects the psychological and spiritual experiences of individuals as they move through life, we are on very safe ground to apply it to the dimension of life that we call sales.

Professional sales, like movies, have a villain. The villain in a movie isn't always a person. It can be a situation or outside force that affects the hero adversely. That's the same in sales. Too often salespeople think of the villain as the obstacle to making a sale, as opposed to outside forces that are hindering the customer's success.

And similar to movies, professional sales have a director and an executive producer. In professional sales, the director is the salesperson. It's their role to lead the team to create a positive buying experience. The executive producer provides the organizational resources and support to make it happen.

Finally, professional sales have a crew behind every successful engagement. In today's complex world, very rarely can one close a sale on one's own. It's a team effort that may require the involvement of finance, account management, operations, technical support, customer service, and a host of other functions within an organization. Imagine making a movie without experts in filming, costumes, editing, locations, music, and mixing. If you want to create an award-winning buying experience, then you need the collaboration of a top-notch crew made up of your internal stakeholders.

When you put this all together, you have a methodology that follows a sequence:

1. You show up in your customer's world, understanding that you'll be a better listener using the hero's journey archetype to assess their situation. You are **story listening** to figure out the plotline of their story. Once you've figured it out, you decide if you can be of help in their transformation.

2. You pivot to **storytelling** by reaching into your story library to share a success story that will enable you to win the customer's confidence and emotional engagement. When they are immersed in a story with a hero that is similar to them and that overcame obstacles similar to what they are facing, they realize you actually have the special resource to help them become heroic in their own story.

3. You and your customer now move on to **story making**. You, or a strategic account manager, are the director that will guide your company's intervention. Your new customer is the main character. In alignment with their goals, the director manages both their cast and your crew.

Before we dive deeper, I would like to tell you a bit of my own story. No, it hasn't been optioned yet for a movie, but I think it will give you insights about why being a professional salesperson is so important to me and why I want to share the lessons and tools that I have learned and created.

# Lost until I Found Sales

It was 1:30 a.m. in late November 1981. Saturday night in the city had turned into Sunday morning, and the guy in the back of my cab was not what you would call talkative. That's okay. When you drive a cab, you pick up all kinds. Some want to talk. Some don't. You follow their lead. Read and accommodate the customer. Assure them you are taking the fastest, most cost-effective route. Nail that combination, and you usually get a decent tip.

The rain was really pouring down. The windshield was getting pounded, and the wipers were working furiously. We arrived at the customer's destination, and the next thing I saw is the back of his black hoodie as he bolted out the door and disappeared into the downpour. Are you kidding me? In two years of driving a cab, that had never happened. Drunks, prostitutes, gang members, doctors, lawyers, and big city bankers—everybody always paid the fare.

Sitting speechless behind the wheel, I stared down the street at the fleeing man. He had no idea I was in the middle of a nonstop seventy-two-hour shift, popping caffeine pills every few hours to keep awake. He didn't know I needed every last dime from every last fare to hand over to a landlord who had handed me an eviction notice. Something snapped in me, but in a good way.

I managed to cobble together enough to pay my landlord, went home, and slept for hours. When I finally woke up, I was still exhausted. I was nineteen, and looking around my tiny apartment, all I saw were the cardboard boxes and milk crates that I used as furniture. There were only two choices for me. Stay where I was or get educated and fulfill my dream of becoming a businessman. As Kevin Costner playing Roy McAvoy in the movie *Tin Cup* says, "When a defining moment comes along, you define the moment, or the moment defines you."

Going back to university to get an education eventually gave me access to the world of sales and entrepreneurship. In my second year of university, I created an orientation guide for first-year students. I put in all the hints, tips, and checklists I wished I had when I was a freshman. Then I went to retailers who wanted to reach the university market and sold them advertising spaces in my publication. This is when I was introduced to the world of professional selling and began to learn the language and concerns of business owners. More doors in sales opened, and I began to see clearly how sales was a lot like driving a taxi—helping someone at point A in their business or career to get to point B. No matter the circumstances, it meant always putting the customer first. Along the way I learned ways of increasing perceived value. I learned about generating repeats and referrals. I gained inner strength, confidence, and self-respect.

Little did I know that all this personal development would lead me to the best relationship-building call of my life when I attended a church conference in October 1985 and worked up the courage to approach a strikingly elegant woman. When you meet the person you know you want to build a life with, it's easy to look back and see how that defining moment was shaped. Even in the middle of a dark night filled with howling winds and torrential rain, all I knew was I needed to be a hero.

Strategic selling is like a business marriage. And like marriage it teaches us many things, but nothing more important than the power of commitment. In business and life, it's astonishing to see what two people from any background or any walk of life can accomplish when they join forces and agree that they are on this journey together for the long haul.

For me the real legacy of my career in professional sales has nothing to do with achievement awards, income, and bonuses. As a former cabbie who became a committed sales professional, the real joy is never just the destination. It's the journey that includes more than thirty-two years of a wonderful marriage and helping thousands of others see sales as an honorable profession.

I'm Adrian Davis, author, speaker, proud husband, and father. Former cab driver.

# The Journey Continues

As I embarked on my hero's journey, I discovered the world of selling and immediately knew I was born to sell. I read the stories of others who were successful in sales, and it was the first time I experienced career clarity. I felt valuable as a salesperson. I wanted to operate at a higher level. I wanted to be a professional salesperson. I wanted to enjoy the autonomy and the success I read about. Others did it. I felt deep within me that I could do it. At the same time, I was aware that sales was not considered an "honorable" profession because of the false belief that a truly effective salesperson operates unscrupulously. Therefore, I resolved to create a couple of life-defining goals. First, I would pursue a career in sales. It's my passion and purpose. Second, I would prove that the most successful sales professionals are the ones who operate with honor and integrity.

*One of my life-defining goals was to prove that the most successful sales professionals are the ones who operate with honor and integrity.*

That was many years ago, and I've been in sales ever since. I became a representative for a leading global CRM company and was successful at what I did. The more successful I became, the more my company brought in other reps and gave them part of my territory. The interesting thing was that as my territory grew smaller, I became even more successful. It seemed paradoxical. My territory was shrinking, but my earnings were doubling every year. Why? I realized that my shrinking territory forced me to focus on who to sell to and how to sell. Circumstances forced me to create more value for my customers. After reducing my geographic territory several times, my employer then asked me to focus solely on the telecommunications industry. That's when my sales really took off. It wasn't long until I was on the radar of other companies.

Along the way I realized that I was selling in a different way than most of my peers. This led me to study my own actions and those of other highly successful professional salespeople. I started my own consultancy with a team and partners, and we share sales processes and growth strategies with chief executives and sales leaders all over the world. I named my company "Whetstone," based on a symbol that has great meaning to me.

A whetstone is a fine-grained stone used with water for sharpening cutting tools. Stephen Covey, in his highly acclaimed book, *The Seven Habits of Highly Successful People*, emphasized the necessity to stop and sharpen the saw in order to improve productivity. The God of the Hebrew Bible states, "If I whet my glittering sword … I will render vengeance to mine enemies" (Deuteronomy 32:41). Your customers are engaged in battles of their own. They need swords, tools, or whetstones as special resources to help them in their battles. More on that later.

Whetting the edge of tools is also addressed in Ecclesiastes, where it states, "If the iron be blunt, and he do not whet the edge, then must he put to more strength: but wisdom is profitable to direct" (Ecclesiastes 10:10). In other words, if the edge of a tool is dull, one must apply more effort. With wisdom one realizes it's better to take time out to "sharpen the saw" in order to be more productive.

At Whetstone we are clear that we are not the hero. The Whetstone metaphor is perfect. The stone symbolizes timeless principles and core philosophies upon which great businesses are built. Water symbolizes knowledge and insight, which are constantly flowing and being replenished. A dry stone will damage the edge of a tool, whereas a wet stone reduces friction, resulting in a sharper blade that remains intact. Our company name represents sharpening a company's edge while simultaneously reducing the friction.

I reinforced the company name with a logo that represents the shift from "me-oriented" thinking to "we-oriented" thinking.

The gray M sits below the vibrant blue W. The M is constricted and unable to grow. The W is expansive and open to possibilities. The W sits on top of the M to show that we all start out with me-oriented thinking. It's only as we mature that we realize that real growth and purpose emerge when we embrace an interdependent world. We can only win when others win. More specifically we can win only *after* our customers win.

I also learned the importance of having strong collaborative partners. Two partners have been particularly important to the success of Whetstone. The Strategic Account Management Association (SAMA; www.strategicaccounts.org) provides critical training to strategic account managers in leading companies. I have the honor of being a member of its faculty and teaching the foundational course in strategic account management. I am also a principal partner with the Summit Group (www.summitvalue.com), a global sales performance improvement company that helps international customers in value-creation journeys and optimizes sales performance through consultancy and customized training.

# Your Brain on Stories

When you were reading my story, what did you feel? What were your takeaways? Did my story enhance my credibility? Did it give you a window into my personality and why I love sales so much? Did you feel empathy for me? Did you want to keep reading to find out more?

That's the power of stories. Neuroscientist Paul Zak has proven that stories are important to humans not simply due to psychology, but more importantly because of chemistry. According to Zak, stories modify the chemistry of our brains. In his epic short video entitled "Empathy, Neurochemistry, and the Dramatic Arc (Future of Storytelling)."[3] Zak explains how before and after listening to a short story about a father and his child named Ben, subjects had blood samples taken. They found that the brain produced two interesting chemicals. The first was cortisol. Cortisol is a stress hormone, and it's responsible for focusing our attention on something important. As the hero is in the pit of despair, our brains experience distress and release cortisol, forcing us to pay even more attention. The second chemical released was oxytocin, which is associated with care, connection, and empathy. His profound finding was that people's behavior

---

3    Paul Zak, "Empathy, Neurochemistry, and the Dramatic Arc," FutureofStoryTelling.org, accessed February 8, 2023, https://futureofstorytelling.org/video/paul-zak-empathy-neurochemistry-and-the-dramatic-arc.

would change depending on how much cortisol and oxytocin were released into their bloodstream. They would become more generous and charitable in very predictable ways.

As we listen to stories and empathize with the hero, our brains release oxytocin, the hormone responsible for social bonding. The release of oxytocin creates a willingness to partner. Stories reduce the friction of empathizing with others. History shows us that those men and women who have made the greatest changes in the world are those that understood the importance of creating connection through empathy.

Our brains use storytelling to attempt to explain the world around us—most importantly how others think (Zak calls this the theory of mind) and to make predictions about what will happen next. That's the only way we can feel safe. For the brain to explain the world around us and ensure our safety, it casts us as the protagonist in the stories. The brain makes us the hero in the stories we hear so it can sample alternate realities and better understand the potential situations we may one day face. Because its primary objective is to keep us alive and avoid suffering, the brain constantly puts us in the position of the main character to allow us to explore alternative actions and subsequent consequences, while it constantly tries to figure out how to keep us alive and successful.

Stories help our brains make sense of events. The more stories that we have in our memories, the more patterns we have at our disposal to make sense of our experiences. Those stored patterns help us understand the relationship between cause and effect.

Every human being lives out their life as their own personal movie. Each person interprets events in life as a cohesive story centered on themselves as the main character with logical cause-and-effect relationships. It's how we mature and how we understand the world. It also is the reason we crave stories. The brain loves stories because, according to cognitive neuroscientist Dr. Carmen Simon, it loves the relationship between cause and effect.[4] The more examples of cause and effect the brain receives, the better it can help us understand and navigate the world. And, when something happens that it hasn't experienced before, it is better able to provide an explanation because of these past experiences.

On the other hand, what the brain hates is when something happens that has no explanation. This causes a sense of panic, as the brain is unable to predict what will happen next and safely navigate us to our destination. When the twin towers fell in New York on September 11, 2001, it was a shocking day for all of us. We were having trouble wrapping our minds around the events that were unfolding. On the news on a major cable network, the anchor expressed that the entire nation, in fact the entire world, had "gone into shock." He then made a statement that I have remembered to this day. He said, "Shock is when experience outstrips narrative." That is so powerful. When the brain encounters something that it can't make sense of, it goes into shock. It is unable to process cause and effect. Consequently, it is unable to direct us.

Playing the role of the main character in our movie is great until we try to communicate with someone who is playing the role of the main character in *their* own movie. Now, we have a subconscious conflict. In our movie we are the hero. But in our customer's movie, they are the hero. Subconsciously, our brains tell us that we must be the hero. Instinctively, we are motivated to come in and save the day. We want the customer to tell us their problem so that we can swoop in, solve the problem, and reinforce our mental model of our heroic status.

---

4    B2B Decisions Labs, "Explore the Science," accessed February 8, 2023, https://b2bdecisionlabs.com/explore-the-science/.

This inner conflict presents a critical challenge to the traditional selling process. The conflict arises over who owns the heroic role. Both the customer and salesperson subconsciously see themselves as the main character in the movie. You can assess if you are playing the hero role instead of your customer by asking yourself the following questions. If you answer yes to any of these three questions, you are imposing your heroic role and pushing your heroic solution into your customer's movie and hijacking the role of the hero.

- Do your presentations begin with "helping" your customer understand who you are, how big you are, how long you've been around, and all the companies that have chosen to do business with you?

- Are you doing the talking instead of listening?

- Do "I," "we," and "our" words dominate your conversation?

Remember that the hero is the main character and actor of the story. In any change effort, the main character is the person who has a strategic goal that is being jeopardized and who must act to evade tragedy and obtain the goal. The goal is being jeopardized by external forces that bring unexpected change—change that is outside of the hero's control. This is the villain in the story (more on this later). In this conflict between the hero and the villain, a question arises—how much does the hero really want the goal? If the hero wants it badly enough, they will dig deep and do whatever they must do to overcome the obstacle.

Our subconscious brain insists that we are always the main character in our own story. Take the movie *Elvis* for example. There's a clip in that movie where Elvis says that when he was a boy, he was a dreamer and would read comic books. He was always the hero of all the comics he read and the hero in the movies he watched. I think this is a fantastic clip because, like Elvis, it's what we all do all the time.

Stories are about individuals. Joseph Stalin, a ruthless leader of the Soviet Union from 1922 until his death in 1953, is estimated to have killed as many as twenty million people. He is frequently credited with saying that the death of one is a tragedy, while the death of millions is a statistic. There's deep insight in that statement. If I tell you about the death of millions from war, it sounds bad. But if I tell you the story of a single mother, who was doing her best to keep her family together and then was taken away and tortured, you might weep. In terms of moving people to action, we can't talk about what happens to millions. We have to talk about what happens to one person, because our audiences empathize when they hear the story of somebody like themselves.

What stories do is immerse us in somebody else's world. While the story is being told, we stop being ourselves and become the protagonist of the story. At the end of the story, we come out with a different perspective and understanding. In professional sales we immerse ourselves in the hero's story, in their journey.

*Great stories follow a dramatic arc. Joseph Campbell called this the hero's journey. Understanding how this journey relates to life and sales is great insight. Let's talk a bit about what makes up a hero's journey.*

# CHAPTER 2

# THE HERO'S JOURNEY

*A hero is a person who says yes to the adventure.*
**—Kendra Levin, teacher, coach, author**

'd like to quickly define several terms that have been carefully chosen to be both memorable and meaningful. These are all components of the hero's journey and will be talked about in depth later in the book when I show you how to complete three important forms:

- The Hero's Journey: Discovery Storyboard

- The Hero's Journey: Success Storyboard

- The Hero's Journey: Action Storyboard

## The Hero

The hero is the main character and decision maker. In general the key decision maker is the economic stakeholder responsible for strategic organizational objectives with authority over company resources in order to achieve these objectives. The hero is a person, not a company.

Companies are systems without feelings that are programmed to reject systemic changes. People feel deeply, and when they feel deeply enough, they will change anything and everything.

It's also important to understand that in professional sales, the hero is not simply someone who holds the purse strings and can sign a check. That's their secondary function. The primary function of the hero is to achieve something strategic for the organization. They've been entrusted by the organization to accomplish important goals and been given a team of people and resources to make that happen.

You can't always immediately recognize a hero. I remember one of my earliest public presentations, which was a keynote for about two hundred people. There was a man at the back of the room who sat stock-still and expressionless throughout my entire presentation. I was telling stories and jokes, asking questions, and doing my best to make my talk interactive. He just sat and stared, so I ignored him because I did not want him to put me off my groove. At the end of my keynote, this man wasted no time coming to the front and lining up to speak with me. He gave me his card, and within a matter of weeks, I met his team, and we began working together. I was convinced he wasn't the least bit interested when in fact he was absorbing the stories I was telling and seeing how the principles I was sharing could apply to his hero's journey.

## THE GOAL

What's the strategic goal of the hero? What do they want in the long run? Many salespeople like to ask the question, what keeps you up at night? I suggest starting with a very different approach with questions such as why do you get up in the morning? What are you trying to accomplish? How will your organization be different three to ten years from now as a result of your specific contribution?

# The Villain

It's very hard for us to think beyond ourselves, but if we are going to create compelling value, it's critical to see the bigger picture. Who or what are the adversarial forces that could jeopardize the hero's goal? In the movie *Captain Phillips* (based upon the true story of Captain Phillips), pirates strike unexpectedly and overtake the captain's ship. The captain and his crew are completely unarmed. The captain must use all his resources and fortitude to outsmart the villains. If you want to understand how powerful villains can derail a hero's quest (and see incredible acting), *Captain Phillips* is a great movie to watch.

Think of industry-level forces and trends that are inexorable and completely outside of the hero's control. Examples of villains are COVID-related disruptions, inflation, supply-chain turmoil, demographic shifts, artificial intelligence, transmigration (e.g., Amazon entering unrelated industries to completely disrupt how value is delivered), 3D printing, war, and more. These are external shocks that change and shape entire industries.

Many sales professionals think in terms of "the pain" the hero is facing because this is what they know and what they can solve. *The villain is different because these forces are completely outside of the hero's and sales professional's control.* This is a critical distinction because if it's a problem that is within the hero's control, the hero will have a sense that when they're ready, they will fix the problem. Villains, by virtue of being adversarial and beyond the hero's control, force the hero into a sense of being vulnerable. Suddenly, they realize this is something that can strike them at any time with devastating consequences. This anxiety forces the hero to prioritize fixing what is in their control in an attempt to successfully navigate the threat of the villain.

As Andy Grove, former CEO of Intel, said, "Only the paranoid survive." External, adversarial forces trigger a healthy paranoia in leaders. They also bring these leaders to the humble realization that as the world changes around them, they may need some outside help to adapt their plans. Now before you rush in to help, it's critical that you realize that you are equally helpless to conquer villains. That's not your purpose. Your purpose is not to conquer the hero's villain, but to make the hero stronger.

## The Flaw

What's the internal weakness or gap between what is and what's desired that must be addressed given the adversarial changes in the industry? In the movie *White Tiger*, the protagonist is born into a subservient class in India and can only dream of being in service to a master. When he finally realizes his dream, he comes of age and through a series of experiences resolves his flaw of naivete.

In business the flaw is usually a business process and/or infrastructure that has become part of the hero's status quo. Invisible in nature, it may be something that worked before but is not working now. For example, when I was with Portal Software, one of the things we loved to do was fly key stakeholders to Silicon Valley. We would create a powerful experience that resulted in an almost

*Your purpose is not to conquer the hero's villain, but to make the hero stronger.*

100 percent win rate. This became an entrenched way of closing major deals. Had the global pandemic hit us at this time, one of our major strengths would have instantly become a weakness. If major customers were unwilling or unable to travel, the jewel of our sales process for major deals would have been rendered useless.

That's how the flaw works. It's so ingrained in the process that when the world changes, it's hard to see it. Fundamentally, the flaw is below the surface. It's actually a belief system that holds the current infrastructure and processes in place. If these are deeply held beliefs, you will face a wall of resistance by the majority of stakeholders. That being said, addressing the flaw is your real value. The future belongs to those who can shift from "problem solving" to "problem finding." Are you able to step back and analyze your customer's holistic situation and anticipate how their future will unfold? Can you see your customer's blind spots? Remember, people don't know what they don't know. As you look out into the future and within your customer's processes and infrastructure, are you able to see what your customer can't see?

## The Pit of Despair

It was Alfred Hitchcock who said, "The terror is not in the bang, only in the anticipation of it." This master storyteller made a living terrorizing people, but his statement provides insight for much of life. We dread something because of what we think it will be like instead  of what it is in reality. That's why the status quo has so much stickiness. The pain of the thought of changing is so great that it paralyzes the customer from acting. Physiologically, a small almond-shaped cluster of cells called the amygdala, which helps regulate our emotions, hijacks our thinking. According to the medical experts at Healthline,

> The symptoms of an amygdala hijack are caused by the body's chemical response to stress. When you experience stress, your brain releases two kinds of stress hormones: cortisol and adrenaline. Both of these hormones, which are released by the adrenal glands, prepare your body to fight or to flee.
>
> Together, these stress hormones do a number of things to your body in response to stress. They:
>
> □ increase blood flow to muscles, so you have more strength and speed to fight or flee
>
> □ expand your airways so you can take in and use more oxygen
>
> □ increase blood sugar to provide you immediate energy
>
> □ dilate pupils to improve your vision for faster responses
>
> When these hormones are released, you may experience:
>
> □ rapid heartbeat
>
> □ sweaty palms
>
> □ clammy skin
>
> □ goosebumps on the surface of your skin

An amygdala hijack may lead to inappropriate or irrational behavior. After an amygdala hijack, you may experience other symptoms like embarrassment and regret.[5]

If there's one thing that can propel the customer to take action to leave the status quo, it's the anticipation of the pit of despair that will result if no action is taken. The pit is a terrifyingly uncomfortable place to be, and that's a good thing. The pit is the anticipated disaster if the business does nothing. The anticipation of the pit creates tension, and if that tension is allowed to build, it can lead the customer to take action to climb out or avoid the pit altogether.

The hardest thing for a sales professional to do is to allow the customer to feel and absorb the pain of the pit instead of attempting to ease the pain. Most sales professionals are so optimistic that every time the customer feels the least bit of discomfort, they want to swoop in and save the day with the answer to what's causing the customer's discomfort.

But that's the exact opposite of what they should be doing. Let the customer wallow. Let them see their coming misfortune in their mind's eye and soak in the anticipated misery. The pain of staying the same has to become so great that they want to move out of the pit. Remember, change is painful. Unless the pain of staying the same exceeds the pain of change, they will always choose to remain the same.

---

5    Kimberly Holland, "Amygdala Hijack: When Emotion Takes Over," Healthline. com, updated September 17, 2021, https://www.healthline.com/health/stress/ amygdala-hijack.

# The Special Resource

The special resource is the best solution your company can implement to help your customer get out of the pit of despair. This occurs by addressing the pit of despair with your tailored and relevant special resources.

The two key words here are "tailored" and "relevant." Too often the sales professional is immersed in the virtues of their solution and assumes they're the best game in town. They believe that what they put forward to the hero is going to be accepted, but that's not necessarily true. According to Rational Choice Theory, people will perform a cost-benefit analysis in order to choose between options.[6] Therefore, what matters is not what you do as much as what you do differently and why that matters. What is it that you do that your customer can't find with another alternative solution? Why is that better for them? More often than not, the differentiation is not going to come from the product. It's going to come from the depth of understanding you have of the customer's situation and how you uniquely combine your capabilities to address the hero's specific challenges.

The idea of getting your perspective to shift from its natural orientation of being the hero to engaging as a special resource is the central thrust of this book. This shift requires entire teams to go against their natural and established pattern of participating in stories as the main character. If you're a leader, this is about moving from

---

6    Wikipedia, "Rational Choice Theory," updated January 30, 2023, accessed February 8, 2023, https://en.wikipedia.org/wiki/Rational_choice_theory.

"problem solving" to "people solving." It takes real effort, coaching, and reinforcement for your people to overcome their egos and to see the world through the eyes of their customers. As their leader, you have the challenge to get the team comfortable with ambiguity. We're far more comfortable understanding the world from our own perspective. Putting our own perspective on the back burner and understanding the world from someone

*The idea of getting your perspective to shift from its natural orientation of being the hero to engaging as a special resource is the central thrust of this book.*

else's perspective can be unsettling—especially if while we are trying to understand how our customer's world is being disrupted, our world is simultaneously being disrupted. No matter what happens in the future, there will always be a role for those special resources who find ways to help others achieve their most important goals in a world of growing uncertainty.

## The New World

As a result of your optimal intervention as the special resource, how does the hero win and how is the hero transformed? In the new world, the hero should emerge with new capabilities that will transform their business. They should be

able to do business in a whole new way. They should have different competencies. Ideally, they should be able to create a superior customer experience for their customers. As a result of your special resource, they are capable of doing more. Change has happened.

Your solution should be compelling. Below are six attributes you should consider to determine whether your solution will be pivotal for your customer.

## PLUGGING IN TO THE SOCKET

I use the acronym SOCKET as a guide for designing a robust solution for customers. For the ideal gourmet solution, think of your solution and your customer's organization connecting like a plug in a socket.

**S—Strategic.** Does your solution impact your customer strategically? Does it help them deliver greater value to their customers?

**O—Over Time.** Is your solution delivered as a short-term transaction, or is it something that your customer will need to work with you over time to achieve?

**C—Combined Capabilities.** Are you relying on a single product, or have you combined and configured multiple capabilities that cannot be easily replicated?

**K—Key Performance Indicators.** Does your solution move the needle on your customer's KPIs?

**E—Embeddedness.** Will your solution be integrated into your customer's operations and increase switching costs?

**T—Transformational.** Will your intervention fundamentally change your customer's organization by enabling them with new capabilities?

Remember the Strategic Account Management Association (SAMA), the organization I talked about early in this book? It is an excellent example of new world transformation. The villain in its case was the pandemic and ensuing economic lockdown. SAMA's strength was its ability to bring account managers together in person and create a real network. In-person training was its main revenue source. When the pandemic struck, this strength became a weakness. At first SAMA leaders thought they would just wait it out, but as time went by with no end in sight, they became nervous that their revenue stream would dry up.

Together with our partner Valkre (the leading software platform for key account management), I facilitate SAMA's foundational strategic account management program. We approached SAMA and suggested that we could do the training virtually and be equally effective. They were initially reluctant because they thought virtual training would be off brand, but we were able to convince them that it could be done. Participants loved it. Everyone was surprised at the value that could be delivered virtually. As a transformational bonus, not only was SAMA able to bring people from around the world together in ways it had never done before, but it has now added a variety of virtual training programs in addition to in-person. Find out more about SAMA at http://strategicaccounts.org.

Before we talk in depth about the how these concepts impact your sales process, let's step back for a moment and establish what genre is most suitable for you. Let's look at the buying experience and its relationship to professional sales and account management. And let's continue to have some fun with our movie analogy.

# CHAPTER 3

# THRILLER, ROMANCE, OR HORROR

## DIFFERENT GENRES OF THE BUYING EXPERIENCE

*There is no greater power on this earth than story.*
**—Libba Bray, best-selling American author**

I magine you go to a movie that you've been told is an action flick. Instead, it's a romantic comedy, a genre that you're not inclined to embrace. You might be disappointed and even leave because it doesn't fit with what you like in a movie. In fact, it might not matter if it's a truly great romantic comedy. It's just not your cup of tea.

Gaining and retaining customers can be a similar experience. What I consider an ideal customer may not be ideal for you even though we're competitors in the same industry. It has to do with both the customer's DNA and our DNA. For example, maybe you're part of a fast-paced, get-it-done-now, shoot-from-the-hip organization. In contrast your customer is disciplined, thorough, and conscientious. If they work with you, they might become frustrated because you'll be disruptive to their organization and culture. Another company that is similar to you would find doing business together a marriage made in heaven because you align so well with them. It's important to know the dynamics of an organization so you value each other and move in lockstep. Even if a company is not an ideal customer, you can do business with them. You just need to proceed with caution.

# Fast-Food versus Gourmet-Food Customers

When I work with sales teams, I use the following analogy to talk about differences in customers. *There are fast-food customers and gourmet-food customers.* One is not better than the other. It's just a completely different buying experience with different buyer expectations. For fast food, you pull up to a drive-through window, and the products and prices are clearly displayed on the menu. You pick what you want, pay the appropriate price, and off you go. You don't start negotiating prices or ordering custom items, because there may be twenty people in line behind you with the expectation that everyone will only spend a few minutes per transaction. The fast-food supplier expects this transaction will be done in two minutes or less so they can serve another twenty-nine customers per hour. If you're taking forty-five minutes with your order, it's not a good fit.

Fast-food customers are not going to value the extras, and that may even include efforts to enhance the relationship. A good friend of mine, for example, is very careful about picking dry cleaners. She has very high expectations. She recently found a great dry cleaner who turned her shirts and suits around very quickly and really did a great job. One day this dry cleaner started asking her personal questions and wanted to treat her like an intimate friend. My friend did not want this level of intimacy; she just wanted a dry cleaner. Even though the service was good, the dry cleaner was trying too hard and going too far in a transactional relationship. My friend switched dry cleaners.

Fast-food suppliers are not restricted to product companies. They can also be service companies. Not long ago I saw a billboard from RE/MAX, a very successful international real estate company, that simply said, "Relax. We've done this a million times!" I thought it was brilliant. That's what fast food means. It means we do this thing all day, every day. We're experts in it. When you pull up to the window and place your order, you're in great hands. You're going to get exactly what you're looking for, and we're going to deliver it competently every time.

That's not gourmet, though. Gourmet means that the supplier may have never done this before, but they know they have the competence to do it. They're going to work with you to tailor their solution so that it exactly delivers what you need, and they are going to charge accordingly.

My company has a mix of fast-food and gourmet customers. Our decision to serve both kinds of customers is based on a very deliberate strategy for growth and profitability. I recommend looking at your strategy, what you want to accomplish, and what you bring to the market to determine whether you want to sell fast food, gourmet, or a mixture. As a general rule, the eighty-twenty rule applies. Eighty percent of a typical business should be highly optimized with repeatable, automated, well-honed processes, procedures, and templates (i.e., fast food). Twenty percent should be exploratory—delivered by the company's best talent and targeted to the gourmet customer.

Understand that you're not for everybody. What's the right size of organization? What's the best industry fit? What kind of individual do you want to work with? Take a good look at who you've sold to from a historic perspective. What do the data tell you? For example,

70 percent of my customers are athletic, middle-aged men with kids in high school or early university. That's their profile. That's data. When they hear my value proposition, it resonates because I've learned to use language like sports analogies and movie allusions that appeal to them. As a person I am relatable to them.

Another tool we provide to our customers is balanced scorecards to assess a customer based on two types of attributes. We say balanced because first we rate the attributes that make a customer strategic to you. Second, we ask you to score the attributes that are evidence that you are strategic to your customers. Scoring both sides creates an objective mechanism that helps you determine if the customer falls into the gourmet category where it makes sense for you to roll out the red carpet and go that extra mile. The following chart shows a two-by-two matrix that enables you and your team to visually see where you should apply your gourmet efforts or leverage your well-honed core processes.

The ability to objectively score before you dive in too deep helps you get agreement on how this customer fits your profile of an ideal customer. If they don't fit, it doesn't mean you reject them. It just means they're going to fall in a different lane with an appropriate level of attention. If you're a user of Salesforce and you would like to score your customers within Salesforce, search for our Client Scorecard app on the AppExchange (https://appexchange.salesforce.com).

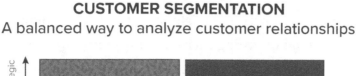

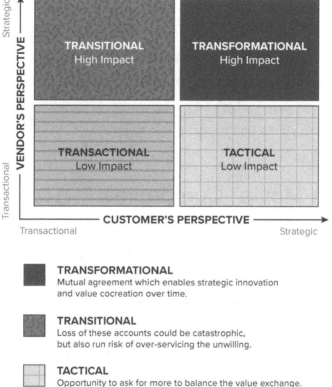

**CUSTOMER SEGMENTATION**
A balanced way to analyze customer relationships

**TRANSFORMATIONAL**
Mutual agreement which enables strategic innovation
and value cocreation over time.

**TRANSITIONAL**
Loss of these accounts could be catastrophic,
but also run risk of over-servicing the unwilling.

**TACTICAL**
Opportunity to ask for more to balance the value exchange.

**TRANSACTIONAL**
Mutual agreement to not explore strategic value
and just focus on the transaction.

What should you look at when you're analyzing a customer fit? You need a sense of industry, size, geographic location, and number of employees—the things that are generally visible online at company websites and through social media. You can also use intelligence tools like InsideView to go a bit deeper to find out more about the executives, latest news, and other secondary background. Once you've done a bit of research, you can begin talking with a potential customer to assess where you suspect they might fall—fast food or gourmet.

This method of getting background is something most professional salespeople do. Generally, they do it more to demonstrate that they have done their homework. Fewer are asking deeper questions to understand what genre of movie the customer represents, or if it is even appropriate for them to exert their sales talent to direct this particular opportunity. Let's take a few moments to look at different genres and how they relate to professional sales.

## "Action-Movie" Companies

When I think of action-movie companies, it reminds me of the first big deal I did when I started Whetstone twenty years ago. I got the chance to meet with a CEO who was struggling with sales performance. We had a discovery meeting, and within an hour he said, "Okay, let's do this. What's the next step?"

I proposed an audit, and he wanted to sign something immediately. I didn't have a proposal, so I told him if he signed a nondisclosure agreement, I could begin. He signed on the spot and agreed to a $25,000 fee. That was the first time that ever happened to me in a first meeting. After he got the audit, he signed up for a $200,000 program (a significant deal to us at the time) to train his whole sales team, develop a process, and create documentation. He placed a full gourmet order because of a great discovery conversation, follow-up audit, and our ability to match his pace.

Similar to a customer in a fast-food drive-through who's in a hurry, if we were not able to keep up with him, we would have been out. He did not suffer fools lightly. Fortunately, we were a start-up company and had the capacity to match his pace. Some organizations could not have moved that quickly. In fact, if he came to us today with the need to rapidly develop a tailored sales system, we couldn't match his pace. We would have to set an agreed-upon schedule that would probably frustrate him. Given his unrealistic expectations, we might have to agree to go separate ways.

Action-movie customers have a very strong bias for action that means you have to adjust your time and processes. Their mindset is action matters more than mistakes because through quick action they can fix mistakes. In contrast, people who don't have that bias for action tend to be more worried about making mistakes. They're intimidated by the obstacles that they see. They're worried about acting too fast because it could be the wrong action.

Here's a couple other observations I have about action-movie companies. First, they are less likely to understand encroaching or emerging villains because their eyes are focused on the prize in front of them. They're going so fast and are so focused that they don't see what's coming up behind them.

Second, action-oriented executives often need to have control. For them, moving from their ordinary, day-to-day world is about losing control of their environment. What they often do is take a success formula that worked in the past and double down on it. They figured out how to be successful but are confused when something new happens and renders their previous formula ineffective. They're thrown into a whole different world, and whatever they did in the past no longer works. In fact, matters often get worse when they double or triple down with their past formula. This situation is totally confusing for them, and they feel despair because they've lost control. They will seek your intervention to regain control.

Third, action-movie companies tend to be less loyal. When you come forward with an intervention, they may rejoice and act like it's the flavor of the month. The minute they get distracted with something else, they'll drop you and go with someone. Their obsession with fast action causes them to quickly pivot to other options.

Finally, professional salespeople need to be particularly astute not to act as if they are the hero with this kind of company. Action-oriented leaders will reject you immediately because they completely see themselves as the hero in their action movie. This can be challenging to many salespeople because they also have an action mindset; they want to be the hero and save their customer.

## "Complex-Thriller" Companies

Many salespeople won't sell to large corporations because it's so difficult to get in and figure out who they should be talking to. These complex-thriller-movie companies may have many gatekeepers and move slowly. A typical sales cycle of six to nine months might extend to more than eighteen months. Additionally, these large organizations often have large budgets, so many sellers may pursue the deal, but only one is going to win. Essentially, it's high risk, high reward—not unlike making a blockbuster film.

What's also difficult with complex-thriller companies is that while you have an economic stakeholder—the main character or hero—there are many other stakeholders who are important and have to be treated as heroes as well. That means we must understand their goals and how the story is unfolding from their perspective. They are part of the subplot and critical to making a sale and having a successful engagement. Often, it's challenging for a sales professional to understand how to manage multiple stakeholders, understand organizational dynamics, and develop coaches that help them understand the politics.

Like a complex mystery, a complex-thriller customer has many twists and turns to the plot. There are more pieces on the board. A large global organization has multiple business units in different geographies competing with different local competitors, pricing strategies, and macroeconomic issues. You have to accept this complexity, see through it, distill it, synthesize it, and then speak very clearly and succinctly about what you've assessed.

Not very many salespeople are able to do this, which means they are essentially pitching in the dark and waiting a long time before they get a response. Good professional salespeople that I've worked with and trained have a mind for this. If you'll allow me to mix my metaphors, they realize this is a gourmet meal and it will take time. A good, slow-cooked meal always does. They're able to sit back and assess the whole situation and come back and say, "Okay, this is what we see, and this is how we believe we can help you." Their assessment brings compelling value and convinces key stakeholders that they will bring additional compelling value if given approval to proceed.

Good professional salespeople put in the legwork. What's important to successfully navigating this mysterious terrain is understanding the key stakeholders, identifying the main character, and aligning with their strategic goals. Before you approach a key stakeholder, do your homework so that when you show up, you can talk to them about their situation, not about your offering, which is irrelevant unless it maps to what they're trying to achieve.

*What's important to successfully navigating this mysterious terrain is understanding the key stakeholders, identifying the main character, and aligning with their strategic goals.*

A professional salesperson also needs to rally all other stakeholders around the bigger strategic goals and show them how they can achieve their personal goals while contributing to the collective accomplishment of bigger, strategic goals. The best salespeople for large, complex companies are strategists. They're strategic in their thinking, and that enables them to successfully engage senior executives. They're captivating because of how they speak, the questions they ask, and the advice they give. That's very different from the traditional transactional salesperson who just wants to talk about their product. That's not going to be engaging to this type of company.

What's also powerful with these types of companies is the villain. The right villain is a uniting force. The bigger and more threatening the villain, the more people unite. *Braveheart,* while not a complex thriller, helps us understand the impact of a powerful villain. In this movie, Mel Gibson plays the legendary hero, William Wallace. Wallace successfully united warring Scottish tribes to withstand the oppression of the English king Edward I. Whenever we face larger villains, we are able to put smaller differences aside. Think of it as a neighborhood where a massive hurricane is about to make landfall. Whatever disputes may have existed between neighbors are put behind them, as everyone works together to pile up sandbags. That's what villains do. They create unity because people put aside their differences to prepare for the onslaught of the villain.

A professional salesperson relates strategic goals to world changes that will impact those goals. For example, how will external forces like inflation, energy costs, war, and food shortages impact your customer's strategic goals? There may be factors that were not on our customers' radar twelve months ago but are now on the horizon with the potential of disrupting their business.

Here's an approach I've used and trained sales professionals to use when approaching new customers when talking about the villain: "We've spent a lot of time in your industry, and we're concerned about some of the trends we're seeing. But we are also seeing some of your peers who are successfully navigating these emerging trends. We'd like to share some of the things we're seeing that are relevant to you and talk with you about what you're seeing and how you're navigating these emerging trends." Some variation of this might work well for you. What's critical is not to talk about your product at this point. What's going to engage them is talking about the forces that are outside of their control that can detrimentally impact their goals.

Any good complex thriller is loaded with clues. The same is true about selling to these types of companies. The salesperson needs to become a detective figuring out what's really going on. One of my customers works in one of the largest global pharmaceutical companies. They face stiff competition, and, unfortunately, that means margins are often razor thin. Fortunately, he learned the critical principles of cocreating value with his customer and managed to get both internal and external stakeholders rallied around navigating industry uncertainty in order to help achieve their strategic goals. The result? He successfully negotiated a $2 billion deal with decent margins (that's billion with a B!).

My customer attributed this win to keeping the team focused on addressing the villain and achieving strategic objectives. Through the process of working collaboratively with his customer, he looked for clues to map out what was really going on. What were the key metrics? What were the key performance indicators that measured success? What direction were they going in? Why were they off track, and by how much? What changed? These were the clues that helped him understand the account before he recommended a plan. Because of his success in negotiating this deal, he's been promoted to lead a strategic accounts team and is equipping them to function at a much higher, strategic level with their customers.

Unlike the action-movie customer, a complex-thriller customer wants you to take time and validate the data that help them succeed. One aspect of clues is that they may shift during the hero's journey. It's vital for the professional salesperson and account manager to be open to shifting changes or new information. A great mystery story works because you don't know "whodunit." Sometimes a salesperson may be so sure of what they are offering and overconfident in their product that they do not dig out the root cause of the problem. We need to be patient and persistent in order to understand the real challenges that need to be addressed. *The key word here: patience.*

One of the stories about patience I like to share is the marshmallow experiment.[7] It was devised by psychologist Walter Mischel in 1965. A group of four-year-old children was put in a room with a researcher who told them that he needed to step out for a few moments. Before he left he gave each child a marshmallow with the instructions that if they did not eat the marshmallow, he would give them another one when he came back. The cameras recorded the children struggling with the decision of whether or not to eat the marshmallow. Some gobbled it up immediately. Others struggled not to succumb to the temptation in order to get two marshmallows. One kid even hollowed out the marshmallow so that it looked like it hadn't been eaten.

The real fascination of this study is the researchers tracked the kids over the next twelve years. They found that those who ate the marshmallow immediately because of lack of patience and self-disci-

---

7    PBS News Hour, "Resisting the Marshmallow and the Success of Self-Control," 9:21, https://www.youtube.com/watch?v=BLtQaRrDsC4.

pline struggled with friends and family. They were more easily frustrated, they were indecisive, and they were disorganized. Many even dropped out of school. The ones who delayed gratification and did not eat the marshmallow excelled in family and friend relationships and school. They were more confident and more self-reliant, and they scored about two hundred points higher in their SAT tests. Their future looked much better than those children who had immediately eaten their marshmallow.

Sales professionals, especially those who are going into big, complex organizations, cannot eat the first marshmallow because it looks like an easy sale. If so, you end up in a transactional relationship. Instead, you need to do proper discovery by talking to a cross section of key stakeholders and be patient. A proper discovery is the key, which means that you need the sponsorship of the hero to go into the organization and talk to the other key stakeholders about what is going on. While you're doing that, you build trust and relationships with all key stakeholders.

You should also begin to gather quantifiable data so that when you come back to key stakeholders, you have substance. It's not one marshmallow; you're after a whole bag of marshmallows now. If you solve this root cause, it's going to impact all the symptoms that the customer is experiencing. This is where you begin to develop a longer-term relationship with these complex organizations.

Account managers play crucial roles in finding clues in an organization. I like to think of them as Sherlock Holmes. They don't make assumptions but go and get the data from key stakeholders. Armed with those data, they can help break through some of these assumptions that may be ingrained in the organization.

# "Romance-Movie" Companies

There are organizations where you just have immediate great chemistry and maintain a special bond over time. These are romance-movie companies and the dream of all professional salespeople.

I've been working with one such company for ten years, and it was love at first sight. The CEO heard me speak and invited me to give a keynote at another organization. She brought along her vice president of sales, who also loved what he heard. This led to a training program that helped them operate at a higher level. Their challenge was that they were getting beaten up by procurement at the big companies they were selling into. Essentially, they were being treated like a commodity, which was significantly reducing their margins.

We needed to switch the mindset and elevate their engagements by demonstrating that they provided real value. This meant getting their small sales team comfortable in front of C-suite executives. We hit bumps in the road during training, which were especially apparent during role-playing. I remember one salesperson who came to me. "Adrian, I can't do this," he anxiously said. "I don't have an education. I can't meet with executives. I don't have the vocabulary." I told him that it wasn't about vocabulary or education. It was about asking questions, listening, and being genuinely curious.

The head of sales had chosen his team very carefully. He knew he had the right people, even if they were struggling. Like a partner in a good romance, he was very supportive, and they started getting in front of the right executives. They began making inroads in terms of positioning their value.

I was so impressed when I saw that through patient application, they mastered the techniques I had shown them. What I appreciate most about this company is their focus on execution. It's not just talk.

They stuck to it with more coaching and training. I saw the competence kick in and how they would support and reinforce each other. They told me one story of meeting with a CIO where they were asking great questions based on their training. The CIO leaned back, took off his glasses, and looked at them. Then he reached into his drawer, pulled out his strategic plan, and transparently shared it. Something happened in that meeting where he just saw the salespeople as sincere and able to help.

When I started working with this customer, they had thirty-five people. Today they are approaching five hundred. They are repeatedly celebrated by their partners (Microsoft, Dell, HP, Ricoh, etc.) with best supplier awards. When I first met them, $40,000 was a significant deal. A few years ago, they closed a five-year, $38 million deal and, recently, a $50 million deal.[8] Because of wins like these, my customer has received significant funding to scale and acquire other companies. And my romance with them continues.

Like a good romance story, a professional salesperson needs to also look closely at the customer—beyond initial appearances. I remember flying out to meet the leaders of this company, and their office was in the basement of an old building. There was nothing attractive about their space. But I was attracted to their character, passion, and genuine nature. Today, they have a beautiful, multi-million-dollar campus to bring customers to, and their business is booming. By the way, the salesperson who won the $38 million deal was the same person who feared he didn't have the vocabulary to talk to C-suite executives. Today, he is well known among all the C-suite

---

8    Alex MacPherson, "Saskatoon Tech Firm Lands $38 Million Government Contract," *The StarPhoenix*, March 3, 2016, https://thestarphoenix.com/business/local-business/saskatoon-tech-firm-lands-38-million-government-contract.

executives in the industry he sells into and leads a team of salespeople tasked with selling into strategic accounts.

Through some follow-up work, I had the opportunity to talk with the economic stakeholder of the $38 million deal and ask him how he made his decision. His answer was profound:

> Our interaction changed us. In the past when we issued an RFP, we would have said, 'We're looking for mousetraps. This is how they should perform. What's your price, and how quickly can you get them to us?' As a result of working with your customer, we changed our whole approach to the RFP and decided that we were going to listen to the experts. Rather than telling them what they should provide to us, we're just going to say what the outcome is we're looking for. Then, we ask them about their approach. If we're trying to get rid of mice, we're going to listen to your ideas. If you tell us to forget about mousetraps and to bring in cats, you're the experts. We're not going to dictate to you what the solution is. We want to unlock the creativity of our suppliers. We issued the RFP so that it was outcome based.

Many sales professionals are frustrated by the abuse they experience in the RFP process. What we see in this example is the fact that sometimes purchasers resort to this approach simply because they don't know a better way. Once they see a better way, they can change.

## "Sci-Fi-Movie" Companies

Science-fiction companies are leading-edge technology companies that are shaping the future with daring innovations. What they need to understand and appreciate is that technology does not sell itself.

Often, their customers have a hard time fully understanding what it can do.

I grew up watching *Star Trek* (the original series) and didn't miss an episode. When my son was ten years old, he watched an episode with me. He laughed out loud at the mediocre special effects. What he didn't realize is that it was all about the story. Back in the day, my siblings and I would immerse ourselves in the story and willingly use our imagination to make up for the lack of special effects. If it's just special effects without a compelling story and good character development, who cares?

An article by Rebecca O'Neill on what makes for great sci-fi movies states,

> A riveting storyline is a baseline for any great film, but it is a huge part of successful sci-fi films. When the writing is phenomenal it makes up for other aspects that might not have been as well developed, such as a lack of special effects or some science that doesn't quite make sense. A great writer will win them over with words and a story progression that will have them on the edge of their seats that will hook them until the very end.[9]

Sci-fi companies need to understand this because they are typically founded and run by brilliant engineers. These engineers are often enamored with their technology; they believe it's so groundbreaking that it should sell itself. They can't understand when there is resistance to adoption. Frequently, we see inferior technology outsell superior technology and retain market dominance because there is a stronger story associated with the inferior technology. Examples

---

9    Rebecca O'Neill, "5 Aspects That Make a Great Sci-Fi Movie (& 5 That Don't)," ScreenRant.com, May 16, 2020, https://screenrant.com/aspects-great-sci-fi-movie-dont/.

include QWERTY versus DVORAK keyboards, JVC's VHS versus Sony's Betamax video, Intel's x86 versus Motorola 68K computers, Sony's mini disc versus compact cassettes, and Sony's Blu-ray versus Toshiba's DVD.

What sci-fi organizations need to learn is to be patient and not focus on what they do but to listen very, very carefully to their customer's story and desired outcomes. Then they need to speak in relevant, precise, and specific ways about what their technology can actually do to help the hero in their very specific situation. This is very difficult for sci-fi organizations. They get so wrapped up in their technology that all they want to do is talk about it and overwhelm the customer with their "special effects." The customer hears about capabilities that have no real value to them and their hero's journey.

What does all this mean to you? It means you may be taking a big risk when selling to the sci-fi genre. The brilliance of science fiction is we have to suspend our disbelief in order to enter into a world that doesn't actually exist. That's the risk in selling to this genre. They are so leading edge that we have to suspend disbelief. We have to understand their vision and subscribe to their passion for the future. The problem is at some point that vision has to be accepted by the market. According to Geoffrey Moore in his best-selling book *Crossing the Chasm*, in order to cross the chasm between early adopters and the early majority, innovators must be able to provide the latter with instant improvement in their productivity.[10] Real and predictable outcomes must be delivered. Hopefully, that's where you come in. While you are excited about the possibilities of your sci-fi client's vision, the real question is how can you help them create a compelling story of value to their customers?

---

10   Geoffrey Moore, *Crossing the Chasm* (New York: Harper Business, 2014).

I have one customer that is leading the way in digital twinning where players in the construction industry can build a whole building virtually before anyone begins to actually construct it. This enables engineers, architects, and general contractors to collaborate on how the building will be built and what needs to be done. In training their salesforce, I advise, "Hold your fire. Uncover more. When you present, don't present everything. Be very, very precise about what you have and how it can help." Failing to do so means they resort to demonstrating features without the context of the customer's story. Without that context, all their potential customer sees is whizbang technology without a clear, outcome-based value proposition.

## "Drama-Movie" Companies

As professional salespeople, we need to see urgency—the drama—that is affecting certain companies. Companies facing drama must experience rapid transformation, or they will either cease to exist or lose the power of their brand. Consider Blockbuster Video. It did not change. Contrast that with Netflix, Amazon Prime, and Hulu, which are now the dominant players. Consider Kodak. It owned photos. Special times were even called "Kodak moments." It did not transform with digital and is now a shadow of its former self. Consider AAA (America's roadside assistance). It was a rite of passage for American parents to give their kids a AAA membership to get directions and get help on the road. These benefits became obsolete with GPS and service contracts, and AAA did not strategically adjust and leverage a brand that had a great reputation in the marketplace.

Remember when I told you that one of the first jobs I ever had was as a taxi driver? Talk about industry changes that were never appropriately addressed. Instead of going on the offensive when Uber and Lyft entered the market, taxi companies failed to provide better service and new offerings. They didn't invest in nicer cars. They didn't invest in training their drivers. They didn't invest in better technology. Instead, they went on the defensive with lawsuits and tried to block emerging industry competitors through regulations. We all know how that turned out.

There's a distinct advantage working with a company undergoing drama, because you can help them figure it out and change. As rapid change becomes the norm versus the exception, drama customers are real opportunities for smart professional salespeople.

# "Comedy-Movie" Companies

As much as we all love a good comedy, for the purposes of applying genres to sales, comedy is the genre of customers that you want to avoid. Movie comedies in general are pure escapism and fluff. After watching a comedy, we don't feel like it changed our life. It's a laugh. But as a professional salesperson, can you afford to spend a lot of time with a potential customer for just a laugh? Let me share some of my own experiences with comedy companies.

We had a potential customer, did our discovery, found out what the issue was, and put together a very compelling proposal. They liked it and signed an agreement for a $250,000 engagement that would drive them forward to the vision they had articulated. A couple of days later, they reneged on the contract, saying they were not going to do it. The clue I should have picked up on was nobody in the organization contradicted the CEO during meetings. In fact, they only spoke up to agree with whatever the CEO said. It was not worth taking the company to court when they reneged on the contract, so we dropped it. The cost of time invested, however, was high. It was no laughing matter, but I did learn my lesson.

Another organization wanted me to work with its account management team. It was a smaller engineering firm and quickly saw how equipping its team with the ability to sell value instead of capabilities could really accelerate its results. After a few meetings, we knew that we could definitely help but asked to be paid 50 percent up front and then 50 percent on the day of the initial training. They agreed, but their credit cards did not go through—three different times! In the past I wouldn't have taken a deposit. I would have gone in, done the work, and trusted the buyer. But I think there are clues that people are not going to be true to their word. They don't have the budget, yet they're presenting themselves as if they can do what they say they're going to do.

I'm pleased to say that these are the only two unpleasant situations I've encountered in my twenty years of running Whetstone. Today, the people we interact with are true professionals, not amateur comedians. I have learned that comedy companies are no joke.

I'd like to add some thoughts here about qualifying budgets. Salespeople are rewarded on closing deals, so sometimes they do not do the level of budget checking required. Here's the problem: if you're not willing to ask tough questions, you're going to get hurt in the long run. The best sales performers ask tough questions up front. Where will the budget come from? Is it coming out of your budget? How much budget have you set aside?

Qualifying budget and fit makes it easier to focus on what's important. In my own career, there was a time when I chased everything and was extremely diligent in following up with everyone. My sales manager pulled me aside and said, "Adrian, you're good. But do you want to know the difference between you and the people who really succeed in this business? The people who make it in this business can smell the deal. You, on the other hand, chase everything."

That was a turning point in my career. I became very careful about my time and whether a potential customer was qualified or not. Budget questions became a qualifier. I remember setting a bar of a million dollars. If a lead came in and didn't have at least a million dollars to address their challenges, I'd pass it to someone else on our team. And I wouldn't be excited about a lead until I could determine if it was real. I would ask about budget right up front. That was an appropriate cutoff point for the multi-million-dollar solutions I was selling. What is an appropriate cutoff point for the solutions you sell?

Salespeople have a quota to reach, but you don't need to close everything to get to that number. The more garbage you can get out of your funnel, the better you'll perform and the more likely you'll be to surpass your quota. As professionals we need to actively work at not becoming overwhelmed. When we are overwhelmed and a lead comes in, the brain doesn't want the lead on a subconscious level. We may not respond quickly, or we may get sloppy. The brain is pushing back.

*The more garbage you can get out of your funnel, the better you'll perform and the more likely you'll be to surpass your quota.*

Be very protective of your time. When that lead comes in, get on it right away to figure out if it's a good, qualified lead. If it is, jump on it. If it isn't, disqualify it and create more bandwidth for yourself. The nature of the engagements you pursue is going to be of a much higher quality because you've created the bandwidth to do quality work. You don't need to close every deal. You need to close the right deals.

# "Horror-Movie" Companies

Horror-movie companies don't respect you. They are disrespectful of your time and payment terms. They're constantly asking for scope creep but don't want to acknowledge that they are asking for something totally different. These are companies we want to avoid or at least learn how to put boundaries around our resources.

Horror-movie companies also are often led by individuals with big egos. Think of the horror movie *Frankenstein*. Doctor Frankenstein's ego was so big that he thought he could create life. In a horror-movie company, everything is basically driven by the leader's ego, which makes transformation difficult.

How do you recognize a horror-movie company before you are actually working with it? A clue would be how it treats its employees. If you look at Glassdoor and see significant negative reviews, that's going to be a major tell. Watch during meetings when you have multiple stakeholders together. How do they speak in each other's presence? Is conversation free flowing? Do they interrupt each other? Do they talk over each other? Do they insult or denigrate each other publicly? These are clues that tell you something is wrong.

If you are working with a horror-movie customer, what can you do to make things better? That's where account management kicks in by having an adult conversation with the customer grounded in a help-me-help-you approach. Here's how the conversation may play out. "Let's do a check to see how it's working for you. What's working and what's not? What do you think we did well as a team? What can we do better? We'd like to share our perspective too and brainstorm together about how we might turn this ship around. Maybe it can't be turned around, but let's figure this out together."

If they're not pulling their weight, you need to call them on it. You need to get them to share their perspective while listening carefully. Because if it's not going well for you, it's probably not going for well for them either. Get them to share their perspective. Don't make it adversarial. Make it collaborative. And there's no shame in firing a customer. Do it graciously. Do it collaboratively. Get to the point where you both agree that not working together might be the best path forward.

No matter what movie genre your ideal customers fall into—action, complex thriller, romance, horror, science fiction, or drama—they still follow a hero's journey. Let's talk a bit about what makes up a hero's journey.

Change cannot happen unless there are individuals who feel the need for change. Two individuals that have key roles in change are the inside-outsider and the outside-insider. Let's take a few moments to understand them.

# ACT II: SALES PROCESS IMPLICATIONS

**CHAPTER 4**

# THE INSIDE-OUTSIDER AND OUTSIDE-INSIDER

*If outsiders know all your business, check your insiders.*
**—Anonymous**

What do *My Big Fat Greek Wedding*, *Get Out*, *Juno*, and *Little Miss Sunshine* all have in common? They were all low-budget indie films that became big blockbusters. They were the movies that nobody in power believed in but still managed to get made. In fact, *Juno* was made on a $7.5 million budget. It had such a low budget that one of the stars took a pay cut to keep costs down. It went on to make $231.4 million worldwide at the box office.[11]

A strategy to get films made and distributed in Hollywood is the same one used by smart professional salespeople—finding and utilizing the "inside-outsider." Imagine you are a writer who wants to fly out to Hollywood to pitch your script. It's a great script but quite

---

11    Tiffany Green, "Best Low-Budget Movies That Became Big Blockbusters," Collider.com, November 4, 2022, https://collider.com/best-low-budget-films-into-blockbusters/.

different from what's being produced right now. In fact, it's so good it could open up a new genre of movies. You are not naive. You know that your odds of getting it in front of risk-averse decision makers are not good.

But you believe that an amazing executive producer or director could become so enamored by the script that they would become your advocate—someone who is part of the movie community, has influence, and also knows that if the industry does not start adopting fresh ideas, big trouble is down the road. Maybe this inside-outsider has a specific director in mind but knows they are more prone to romance, so they advise you to add a love interest. Or the inside-outsider may need to work with you because they know a producer won't buy it because it's too complicated to make. But, like you, the inside-outsider wants change in the movie industry and is going to help shake things up in a knowledgeable way. Their insight as an insider enables them to understand how to navigate change in their specific organization.

# The Inside-Outsider

The inside-outsider concept makes me think about the plot of *Harriet*, a movie about Harriet Tubman. Tubman managed to miraculously escape the evils of slavery by journeying from the Deep South into Canada—a journey that would come to be known as the underground railroad. Despite the miraculous nature of her escape, she was not content. She returned to the Deep South thirteen times in order to free her family and friends. As we watch the drama unfold, it becomes crystal clear that this feat would be impossible for her to achieve by herself. She required the assistance of people on the inside who realized the status quo was evil. She needed inside-outsiders.

Let's put this in the perspective of professional sales and strategic account management as it relates to the hero's journey. True change is an inside job. Ultimately, the hero must be the one who embraces and drives change. Often, however, the hero may not initially see or accept the need for change. The hero may initially block your progress because they have serious concerns about working with your company. That doesn't mean all is lost. The inside-outsider is the initial access point to bring true change to the customer. This is the individual on the inside of the company who realizes the danger of the status quo. Your objective is to win them over to see your special resource as their best chance for successful change so they become your advocate.

How do you find the inside-outsider? In some cases they actually will be the hero or economic buyer because they have a strategic lens that gives them a vision of emerging villains on the horizon and likely are the first in the organization to recognize such villains. It is the presence of villains that drives the need to address flaws in the status quo. The economic buyer is typically a visionary who realizes that the impact of an emerging trend won't be felt for years but will eventually have an impact. They start looking for solutions early in order to begin putting them into place before a negative impact is felt. They understand that an unchecked trend will eventually threaten their goals and potentially their ultimate survival.

Remember, the environment of every business is constantly changing. There is change happening that is outside the control of the hero, and thus their goals are always being threatened. This is the sales professional's opportunity to serve the hero by being the special resource that can pull them through the status quo so that their goals can be reached. That means sales professionals need to understand the customer's industry, how that industry is changing, and how those changes will adversely impact their goals.

Ultimately, you are looking for the executive who has a goal that is being jeopardized by an industry-level change. That is the person who is going to realize that though it may not be today, someday soon the organization will be in big trouble unless they start changing now.

One thing to look for when trying to identify a potential inside-outsider is a recent newcomer to an organization. Typically, for the first ninety days, this new employee is trying to get their head around the status quo and why things work the way they do. Inefficient processes are jarring to them. They are filled with ideas from their previous experiences, and if they don't act on those observations, then they will eventually be absorbed into the status quo.

Users are also potential inside-outsiders. They are trying to get work done and, as a result, when things change and the status quo becomes inadequate, they're often the first to realize the problems.

Regardless of who the inside-outsider is, their purpose is always the same—to prepare the organization to embrace needed change. The inside-outsider is not necessarily your champion—at least not initially. Once you win their trust in you and confidence in your solution, the inside-outsider will become your advocate on the inside and help bring the other stakeholders on board. They accomplish this effectively because of their deep understanding of how their organization operates.

Often, salespeople confuse the inside-outsider with their advocate. This is a very important distinction and worth repeating. *The inside-outsider is the advocate of change, not necessarily your advocate.* They'll listen to you, but be aware that they could be entertaining your competition as well, until you convince them that you're the optimal special resource. Initially, all you can count on from an inside-outsider is their support to change the status quo. That doesn't mean they necessarily support your solution. They just want their organization to move away from the status quo. In reality they may end up supporting another solution. Take the time to ensure they understand how you can help the organization embrace change in a superior way to anything else they are considering.

Once you find the inside-outsider, your job is to get them to see your solution as the best option and your company as the best partner for their change efforts. If you are not the best fit, you should move on and find customers who are the right fit.

An inside-outsider can get you into a company where access would be challenging. One of my customers is a huge and very buttoned-down manufacturer. The company was going through changes and received a recommendation to talk with me about my hero's journey approach. I did a webinar for a few executives and their commercial teams. They loved it. And then nothing happened. They showed no interest in furthering a relationship with Whetstone.

Then, an individual got promoted to enhance key account management capabilities. Suddenly, everything changed. He came and took an account management course with me. I didn't know if my content would be of value to him or the organization because it was introductory, and he was involved in very complex, global customer relationships. He really appreciated the content and sent other people to take the course. We ended up training more than one hundred of their top commercial people with a specifically tailored multiyear program.

> *Once you find the inside-outsider, your job is to get them to see your solution as the best option and your company as the best partner for their change efforts.*

He was my inside-outsider. I would have never ever been able to accomplish what I did without his help. Interestingly, before joining this company, he was one of their customers. He came in with a customer perspective that they were too slow, were too product oriented, and had problems with communication. He also believed that while the market for his company was favorable at the time, it would not always be. He saw the need for his organization to build strategic relationships during this favorable market to prepare for when the market became unfavorable.

Our inside-outsider had the authority to make changes, and we worked collaboratively toward success. Their net promoter scores went up. They successfully negotiated incredible deals. In fact, during a presentation by their CEO to four hundred of their top executives, he called out the great job the key account management team was doing.

Sometimes, even working with an inside-outsider does not get the needed results because they may not be the hero and may ultimately fail in convincing the hero. Recently, I talked with an inside-outsider who understood how important and difficult it is for his organization to change. He warned me to get in front of more senior stakeholders before any training began. In contrast the executive sponsor of the project (the hero) said we didn't need to do this. For whatever reason he did not want to gain greater stakeholder support, and the inside-outsider was unsuccessful in convincing him of the need to do so. When the training began, 50 percent of the people did not show up because there was a competing event they needed to attend.

Working with the inside-outsider is about change management. This is the person that's going to help you not only get into the organization but also be successful in your intervention. They want change and understand how change happens inside the organization. They know who needs to be on board. They know why their organization will face roadblocks.

Sometimes, your original inside-outsider will leave the company. It should not matter. Once you have a community of inside-outsiders, you have sufficient groundswell. The inside-outsider is the initial point of commitment to change and helps get others on board. Then there's enough momentum. There are enough inside-outsiders that even if some leave, you have traction for change. As a bonus the inside-outsider who leaves for another company is now your advocate at a new position. Developing Whetstone advocates from inside-outsiders is one reason we have successfully grown over the years.

## The Outside-Insider

As professional salespeople and strategic account managers, we have something special we can offer the inside-outsider. It is very difficult to accelerate change when most people on the inside don't see a problem with the status quo. Change can be accelerated through the partnership between the person on the inside who realizes the danger of the status quo and someone on the outside who has the solution and creativity to correct the fatal flaw of the status quo.

This special resource becomes an "outside-insider" in order to effectively work with the inside-outsider. That means that although you are on the outside, you have to become knowledgeable about the organization, its history, politics, culture, and the personalities of the stakeholders. Most importantly the outside-insider needs to understand why the status quo works for them, why they would fight so strongly to keep it, and why the status quo must change. They need to know how to balance clarity with empathy so they can become a welcomed truth teller inside their customer's organization. Tactful truth telling often comes down to wrapping the truth in a compelling story.

The outside-insider is often the strategic account manager who is so familiar with the organization that they can coach and guide the customer in terms of how to implement change. Often known as the key account manager, their job is to live inside that account; the best account managers actually see themselves like the general manager on behalf of the account. Even though they are paid by their employer, it's almost like they are employed by the account to be their general strategist. The key account manager is looking at where the customer is currently and what's going on. They understand the significance of external forces and how those forces are changing over time. They understand the internal flaws and the strengths of the account. They are in a position where they can be doing in-depth discovery and ideation with the customer based on the way the market is going.

Strategic account managers need to proactively come to the customer's key stakeholders with strategic initiatives based on what's going on. They need to present their ideas in a way that demonstrates how the customer's world is changing, ideas to successfully navigate these changes, what it means to the customer, and the value it's going to bring to them. Additionally, they are able to collaborate with the inside-outsider about questions about how to communicate it within the organization.

To drive momentum based on outside changes, a typical conversation may sound like this: "We've been studying your industry, and we're seeing some important trends. For example, economists are predicting a recession that is probably going to hit your industry harder than others and may begin impacting key industry players in three to six months. This will be exacerbated by the energy crisis and looming food shortages. We are seeing how this will impact your customers and have a few value-creation ideas that we'd like to run by you."

A strategic account manager is in a constant state of discovery. This is the biggest part of the account manager's job, and it's the foundation for everything else. There's a formal way of doing it. It should be done at least annually or when there's a significant trigger event in the marketplace. Ideation comes out of this assessment and then implementation and execution. There are a different set of discovery questions for account management that focus on the villain, including political, environmental, sociological, technical, legal, and economic factors that are happening. The strategic account manager is always looking at these factors and the capabilities of the organization. They are asking this vital question: *Does my customer have the right capabilities to navigate this changing world?*

Let me tell you a story about one of my customers who sells a commodity. He took the concept of outside-insider and applied it to his customers to go beyond being seen as a commodity. He really understood their business and workflows. He was fully committed to ensuring that they always got their orders on time and achieved this by collaborating with them around forecasting.

Then a new person took over at his account and told him that he had to lower his price, or they would give the business to his competition. They were pushing a huge marketing initiative intended to grow the company fast. My customer told them he could not discount his price as requested because of the value he was delivering. He understood their business so well that he knew the financial impact his contribution was having. He told them he was sorry, but if they needed to, they should go ahead and give the contract to the competition.

Six months later the customer was back apologizing and asking him to take back the account. Apparently, when they started pushing out the new marketing campaign, they couldn't get the product when they needed it, and the extra costs were significant. They had been a loyal customer but deviated and regretted their action. The customer had actually not understood their business as well as the strategic account manager. Now they understand the true worth of their outside-insider.

During COVID and the subsequent breakdown of the supply chain, the role of outside-insiders became even more critical. Those companies with strong outside-insiders had fewer supply-chain issues. We have heard from many companies who got to see their suppliers in a new light. There were some suppliers that proactively stood up and helped them work through the crisis. There were others where it was just an opportunistic relationship, and they weren't there when their customer really needed them. Coming out of the crisis changed how companies perceive their suppliers and which ones they really valued.

In the next two chapters, you will learn about the discovery process and account development. This is specifically aimed at bringing in a new customer. If you would like to learn more about how to improve your and your team's strategic account management skills with existing customers, please contact us at https://whetstoneinc.ca/contact-us/.

# CHAPTER 5

# THE DISCOVERY PROCESS

*The prerequisite of knowledge is curiosity.*

**—Jacques Yves Cousteau, oceanographer, filmmaker, author**

No movie gets made without a discovery process that answers key questions. Is the script good? Is the concept different? What audiences will it resonate with? How experienced is the team? Who is the director? Who is the cast? How will it be distributed and marketed? Where is the money coming from? And this is just the tip of the iceberg.

The same is true in professional sales. The discovery process is at the heart of getting a new engagement. You can't do discovery without talking with people, specifically the key stakeholders who are part of the hero's journey. Just as there are supporting characters in a movie, the hero does not act alone in their journey. There are many stakeholders, but the discovery process focuses on three primary ones: the economic stakeholder, the user stakeholder, and the technical stakeholder. They all have different perspectives and can influence the decision.

While access to information has increased exponentially since I started my career, the truth of the matter is no amount of secondary research can substitute for the insight that can be gained through face-to-face conversations. However, secondary research is critical to prepare you for your initial meeting with your customer. Prior to your meeting with a significant customer, you should do a deep dive into

- Industry trends

- Competitors

- News releases

- Annual reports

- Employer evaluation websites

## Asking Questions

The most important part of the discovery process is the questions you ask and your ability to listen for answers. You need the right approach and questions to gain insights from the stakeholders. Asking great questions gets them thinking about what's wrong. What are the key indicators? What happens if they start going in the wrong direction? What else could happen? Who else is affected?

Having the courage to ask difficult questions goes hand in hand with creating an environment where people feel safe. They realize you're there to help them and are willing to share information. It's like going to the doctor. The doctor starts asking you diagnostic questions, and you give them the information for proper treatment.

I've never found asking difficult questions an issue. I've met people in a first meeting who share information that sometimes may even feel a little bit intimate. Why? Because they're hoping that I can help. They open up because they have a sense of who I am from my demeanor and the sequencing of how I ask questions.

Additionally, people open up when they acknowledge the impending doom that the villain might bring. Remember, a strong villain unites us. You could be a neighbor that I've never spoken to before, and suddenly a hurricane is on its way. We're now cooperating and working together to get ready. Getting answers is a combination of the approaching villain and creating an environment of trust. But at the core, it is asking great questions.

A friend once said to me, "Adrian, the brain is like a racehorse, and questions are like the rider. When you pose a question to the brain, it wants to go to work to find the answer." I've always remembered that statement, and, combined with genuine curiosity and interest, I've observed how a well-phrased and well-timed question will motivate your customer to come up with the answer. I have also created two frameworks to help you in the discovery process.

# Framework One: GPSx2

The first framework is GPSx2, a powerful, simple, and memorable acronym to guide your preparation. No matter how busy you are, you can find ten minutes to think about the questions you should ask in order to gather sufficient information from your customer to help them on their journey. GPSx2 ensures you gather sufficient information to understand their story. There are two Gs, two Ps, and two Ss.

GPS is an initialism for a global positioning system. A global positioning system needs two pieces of data: where you are now and where you want to go. Based on those two data points, it calculates your route. Remember, your customer is the hero, and you are there to assist them on their journey. Think of yourself as their GPS.

**G1:** Goal one is their professional strategic goal.

**G2:** Goal two is their important personal goal.

**P1:** This stands for pressure(s)—the external pressure that is outside their control and can jeopardize the achievement of their goal (i.e., the villain).

**P2:** This stands for problem(s)—the internal weakness within their control that they must address if they are to successfully navigate the change in their external world (i.e., their flaw).

**S1:** This stands for suffering—how the hero will suffer if they do not adequately resolve their flaw (i.e., the pit of despair).

**S2:** This stands for success—the benefits and outcomes the hero will enjoy as a result of working with you to overcome their weakness (i.e., the new world).

GPSx2 is a simple, memorable, and powerful model for listening with intention to key stakeholders. The model begins with goals because goals are the keys to emotion, and the emotional impact of all other elements depend on how they relate to the goals.

# Framework Two: A-SALE

If you're meeting a senior executive and you have additional time to prepare, the second framework I created is called A-SALE. It is more sophisticated and detailed than GPSx2, but both serve the same purpose of getting the discovery information you need for a successful buying experience.

*A: Amenity Questions.* These are questions, like a hotel's amenities, that are designed to make your customer comfortable in your presence. When two people meet each other for the first time, there may be awkwardness. Awkwardness is actually healthy because it's our brain's way of keeping us safe. Strangers represent potential advances forward, but they also represent a potential hazard. Your brain doesn't know if a stranger is there to help or to hurt you. Therefore, it remains on guard until it can determine you are not at risk. The purpose of amenity questions is to create comfort, a "we" space that will enable a richer conversation.

A good example of this initial awkwardness we feel with strangers is my own romance with my wife. When I met her, she was visiting from the UK. We clicked, had a meal together, and then she went back home.

Back in those days, there was no email, and long-distance calls were astronomically costly. So, we wrote letters to each other. We sent and received two letters a week and got to know each other extremely well. I went over to the

> *The purpose of amenity questions is to create comfort, a "we" space that will enable a richer conversation.*

UK to meet her parents and the rest of her family. When I got to spend more time with her, it was actually a bit strange. On the one hand, I felt like I knew her well, but on the other, I didn't really know her since we actually spent very little time with each other. In a sense we were still strangers. We knew each other very well from our letters, but being in each other's presence was novel because we had only spent a few days together when we first met. The additional time we spent together eliminated that initial awkwardness. I proposed to her, and within six months we were married.

I'm so glad email wasn't mainstream back then. We treasure those letters we wrote back and forth. We've raised two successful and remarkable children, built a successful business together, and been very active in our church life. What's most amazing is that we are coming up to thirty-two years of a very fulfilling union. Now that's what I call romance! And it all started as two strangers meeting.

If you're successful winning over a new customer, ideally it will lead to a long and mutually prosperous business union. Use amenity questions to break the ice. One of the best things you can do to create rapport and comfort is to find common ground. With today's social media, you can easily find what or who you might have in common with your customer. In the case of my wife and me, we were both born in England, and our parents came from Jamaica. Although she grew up in England and I grew up in Canada, we have so many similar experiences because of our common culture.

One final point on amenity questions is to use them as a natural transition into your strategic context questions by introducing your objective agenda for the meeting. You might say something like, "For our meeting today, it would be great if we could mutually determine if we are a good fit for each other. To that end, the way I usually hold these meetings is to spend the first part asking you a few questions to better understand you and the second part sharing our relevant capabilities based on what you've shared with us. In terms of the questions I'll be asking, after the preliminary amenity questions, I typically like to start with the bigger, more strategic picture before drilling down on the specific challenges you're facing. Does that sound fair?"

It's important for you to set expectations for the meeting, especially if you're going to be asking strategic questions of senior executives. I have found senior executives love to talk strategically to people who can appreciate that level of discussion. A note of caution, however: your questions have to make sense to them.

The only time I ever received pushback from asking strategic questions to a C-level executive was when I was conducting voice-of-the-customer research on behalf of one of my customers. One executive was ten minutes late. I would have normally rescheduled the meeting, as I have found thirty minutes to be the minimum time needed to get executives comfortable and uncover sufficient information for my customers. In this case, because the executive reached out to me to say she was running late and because it had been so difficult to get on her calendar, I waited for her.

When she came on, I realized we were short on time, and after some brief small talk, I jumped into my strategic context questions. She expressed confusion about why I was asking these questions when she thought the meeting was going to be about her relationship with my customer. I quickly realized my mistake and gave the background, purpose, and agenda for the meeting. She immediately understood and was more than cooperative through the rest of the meeting.

***S: Strategic Context Questions.*** Most sales professionals are good at building rapport. However, once they've established rapport, they typically go to problem-exploration questions prematurely. By doing so they destroy the comfort they just established, because the customer knows they are asking these questions so they can sell their wares. Instead of prematurely going to problem-solving questions, I suggest you go to strategic context questions. Strategic context questions explore the big picture (G1, G2, and P1). These questions do not create suspicion, because answering them doesn't enable you to sell anything. What they do is enable you to understand the big-picture context within which you will provide value.

*A: Attention-Focusing Questions.* Attention-focusing questions are problem-exploration questions (P2 and S1). Use these questions to focus your customer's attention on the part of their business where you can help.

*L: Linkage Question.* Use a linkage question to tie the hero's weakness (P2) to their strategic goal (G1). The purpose of this question is to ensure your customer makes the connection between addressing operational issues with strategic imperatives. Linkage questions trigger a chemical reaction in the brain. G1 stimulates the approach mechanism of the brain, while P2 stimulates the avoidance mechanism. Linkage questions trigger both emotional responses simultaneously as the hero comes to their own realization of the strategic implications of their weakness.[12]

*E: Envisioning Questions.* While attention-focusing questions examine problematic issues, so the hero spends time in the pit of despair, feels uncomfortable, and separates from their status quo bias, envisioning questions flip the switch and enable the hero to fast-forward into the new world. Most importantly these questions enable the hero to see and feel what success (S2) will be like. These questions trigger desire and the approach mechanism.

## One Hundred Questions

Over my career, I have compiled a list of one hundred questions that follow the A-SALE sequence to help professional salespeople in the discovery process. I'd like to share those with you. I hope you'll treasure them. Asking a substantive question at the right time will

---

12    Robin L. Aupperle and Martin P. Paulus, "Neural Systems Underlying Approach and Avoidance in Anxiety Disorders," *Dialogues in Clinical Neuroscience* 12, no. 4 (2010): 517–31. https://doi.org/10.31887/DCNS.2010.12.4/raupperle.

uncover incredibly valuable information. I think at least 50 percent of a great salesperson's success is based on the questions they ask and the information they're able to uncover. Obviously, you are not going to ask one hundred questions, which would overwhelm anyone. Instead, select those that seem most relevant based on your secondary research. Ask the questions in a natural way and in sequence. And most importantly, *listen*.

## AMENITY QUESTIONS (QUESTIONS TO BUILD COMFORT AND CONNECTION)

1. Where were you before you started working here?

2. How did they find you?

3. What was the biggest difference in culture that you noticed when you came here?

4. Do you have a long commute to the office?

5. What do you do to relax and shake off the stress of the job?

6. Do you have children?

7. What are their interests?

8. Have you had a chance to take any vacation lately? What did you do, and where did you go?

9. What are your thoughts on [latest news story]?

10. Share meeting objective and agenda and ask, "Is that fair?" or "Will that work?"

## STRATEGIC CONTEXT QUESTIONS (QUESTIONS TO GET AT THE BIG PICTURE)

### *Industry Dynamics*

11. Tell me about factors that distinguish winners from losers in your marketplace and how they may have changed over the last three years.

12. How do you reduce the bargaining power of customers and suppliers?

13. How do you increase barriers to entry to potential new entrants?

14. Explain the threats and vulnerabilities that you face and how they have changed from three years ago.

15. Discuss what you have learned about the market in the past three years.

### *Value*

16. Who are your customers?

17. Can you describe how you create value and how this differs from your competitors?

18. Can you describe the strengths/weaknesses of your organization?

19. What are your core competencies, and what distinctive or unique benefits do they deliver to your customers?

20. Why do customers buy from you and from your competitors?

21. If you left your company for a competitor, how would you compete against your former company?

22. How do customers come to know about you and your competitors?

## Market Drivers

23. How are your markets defined?

24. How do you think your products and services will change in the next three years?

25. How do you think your competitor's products and services will change?

26. What drives your current market? How does that compare with what will drive your future market?

27. What new opportunities and threats might emerge for you in the coming months and years?

28. What related markets are you choosing not to serve, and why?

## Future Direction

29. Describe the three most important contributions senior management can make to your organization.

30. Where do you want to take your company (goals) in the next three years?

31. How will you achieve your goals?

32. Describe the best-case and worst-case scenario covering the next three to five years.

33. How well do you believe your people "get" your vision?

## *Corporate Profile*

34. What's your mission?

35. What's your recent financial performance? (revenues, profits, market share)

36. What are your core competencies, and what distinctive or unique benefits do your core competencies deliver to your customers?

37. Who are your major customers?

38. How would you describe the value you bring to them?

39. Are they enjoying increasing bargaining power?

# ATTENTION-FOCUSING QUESTIONS (QUESTIONS TO EXPLORE CRITICAL COMPONENTS OF A POTENTIAL ENGAGEMENT)

## *Issue Exploration*

40. What issues are you facing? What else? What else?

41. What's happening now that should *not* be happening?

42. What's *not* happening now that should be happening?

43. Specifically, what do you need changed?

44. To what extent is _____ (an aspect of the solution you can bring) important to your business?

45. How disciplined is your _____ team? Why does this matter?

46. How did you get to this point?

    □ Who was involved?

    □ What happened?

    □ How did it happen?

    □ Why did it happen?

47. How do you know this is a problem?

48. What's this problem costing you?

49. How will resolving this issue affect you personally?

50. What has stopped you from solving this problem before now?

## Impact Exploration

51. What are the implications of doing nothing?

52. Who do you see as your true customer?

53. Who is the end user you're trying to satisfy?

54. What level of support do you have now from your customer(s)?

55. What concerns do you have about the project?

56. What are the risks associated with the project?

57. How can these risks be mitigated?

58. What's the background? Has it been tried before?

59. How will solving this problem help you achieve your strategic objectives?

60. Can you paint a picture of how things will be different or better once the project is completed?

61. Explain how you will know when the project has been successful.

62. What steps will you take to ensure the changes we achieve together will actually remain in place?

63. Where are you leaning in terms of engaging people emotionally versus dictating the final solution?

## Budget Questions

64. Where will the money come from for this project?

65. What will you have to give up in order to pursue this initiative?

66. What's your budgeting cycle?

67. Who will release the funds for this project?

68. What's the basis of your business case for the funding?

69. Assuming you select us, when and how will the contract be finalized?

## Timing Questions

70. Is there an impending event?

71. Does this problem need to be fixed before something else happens?

72. Are there any resource constraints we need to be aware of as we plan the timing of the project?

## Decision-Making Process

73. What internal resources can you use to solve this problem?

74. Is an external solution required? Why or why not?

75. What will happen if you upset the status quo?

76. What do you believe needs to be done before upsetting the status quo?

77. Has something like this been tried before? If so, what happened?

78. Who else cares about this decision?

79. What's the decision-making process?

80. How will you interact with others involved in the decision?

81. How will they interact with each other?

82. What criteria will be used to choose among alternative solutions?

83. Where are you leaning in terms of creativity versus functionality of the final solution?

84. Where would a decision like this usually get blocked?

85. Who do you think can prevent this project from being successful?

86. What steps can you take to ensure the project will be successful?

87. What concerns do you have about the project?

88. What concerns do you have about my company or me?

89. What are the next steps?

90. If you were me, how would you proceed?

91. What process can we all agree to adhere to as we proceed?

### Linkage **Questions**

92. How will addressing this project help you achieve your strategic objectives?

93. How does the project fit into _____ (strategic initiative mentioned earlier)?

94. What strategic value will this project bring to your corporation?

### Envisioning **Questions**

95. Can you paint a picture of how things will be different or better once this project is completed?

96. How will you know the project has been successful?

97. How will your colleagues, customers, and suppliers react when the project is successful?

98. If you could wave a magic wand, what would your situation look like tomorrow when you come into work?

99. When you envision the ideal future, what is it that excites you?

100. If you just hired me on as a VP and wanted to ensure I didn't get caught up in the day-to-day challenges, what picture of the future would you paint to get me engaged?

*A few well-thought-out questions will go a long way to making stakeholders comfortable in sharing a wealth of information.*

In my experience, a few well-thought-out questions will go a long way to making stakeholders comfortable in sharing a wealth of information. "People don't care how much you know until they know how much you care." Thoughtful questions and attentive listening are the ways we demonstrate how much we care. For more information on how to ask questions with more empathy, I recommend *The Seven Cs of Consulting* by Mick Cope and *How to Think Like a CEO* by Debra A. Benton.

Equally important to asking the right questions in the right order and listening hard to the answers is developing relationships with key external stakeholders, whom I refer to as the cast. These stakeholders are critical to you getting an engagement. This means understanding the different roles they play and using a checklist to help you through the stakeholder development process. Let's take a look at how this plays out.

CHAPTER 6

# STAKEHOLDER DEVELOPMENT

## THE CAST

*The fundamental law of human beings is interdependence.*
*A person is a person through other persons.*
**—Desmond Tutu, South African bishop,**
**theologian, human rights activist**

At the end of every movie, the credits roll and roll and roll. In fact, there are so many people acknowledged that movies are now putting trailers for a sequel at the end of the credits to keep people in their seats. Fortunately, customer engagements rarely have that many people involved, but there is often a surprising number of seen and unseen players prior to getting the engagement and then delivering on the proposal.

For the purpose of our movie analogy, we think about the customer as *the cast*. They are your external stakeholders. Developing external stakeholders into your supporters increases your probability of success in making a sale and them having a successful and fulfilling buying experience. Think of your own team—those people who work with you and come together to help make the sale and manage the account—as *the crew*.

Let's look at the cast. First, we must understand the role each external stakeholder plays in decision-making. At the simplest level, they are

1. The economic stakeholders or final approvers—the people who control the budget in order to achieve strategic objectives.

2. The users—the people who will actually use the solution.

3. The technical stakeholders—the people who must manage the risk of introducing a new solution and who are therefore concerned with compliance to company standards. They can be found in organizations such as finance, quality, health and safety, IT, HR, procurement, and operations. You might also have people outside the organization, such as external consultants, who are influencers and who also need to be managed.

The economic stakeholder is typically the hero, because they are the one driving toward the strategic goal. Everyone else in the organization, ultimately, must support and contribute to the achievement of that strategic goal. These other stakeholders are the supporting characters. As you consider the different types of external stakeholders, pay close attention to identifying the inside-outsiders. The inside-outsiders, as mentioned previously in chapter 4, are the champions for change. They are the ones that realize how detrimental the status quo is to the organization, and they also understand how the organization adapts or doesn't adapt to change. Your first order of business should be to ensure they are the champion not just for change, but for your solution. A true inside-outsider who becomes your champion is the key, not only to a successful sale, but also to a successful implementation.

A word of caution! It's important to identify all the stakeholders, even if you know you will not be able to meet with them directly. Many sales are lost because the sales professional suffers from an inflated sense of support because they only analyze the stakeholders they are in constant contact with.

According to Ebsta, a leading relationship-management tool that is embedded in Salesforce.com, more relationships with key stakeholders result in more sales. The following data are based on Ebsta's analysis and insights from managing 1.6 million opportunities on their platform:

- Four to six relationships led to a 19 percent increase in win rates compared to those with just one to three.

- Nurturing seven to nine relationships improved win rates by 14 percent over those with just four to six relationships.

- Opportunities with ten to twelve relationships delivered the strongest win rates at 56 percent.

- Opportunities with a strong ensemble of seven to nine relationships took 58 percent less time to close compared to those in 2020.

- Nurturing four to six stakeholders led to 29 percent shorter sales cycles year on year.

- Highly engaged opportunities took 38 percent less time to close.[13]

---

13   Ebsta, "2022 B2B Sales Benchmark Report," accessed February 8, 2023, https://www.ebsta.com/the-2022-b2b-sales-benchmarks-report/.

Relationships matter! Once you've identified all the stakeholders, your next task is to categorize them according to their degree of political influence and power and their sentiment toward you. Many of my clients find the following chart extremely valuable. By placing power and influence on one axis and positive or negative sentiment on the other, you can create a two-by-two matrix with four quadrants. As a memory aid, I label these quadrants "ABCD."

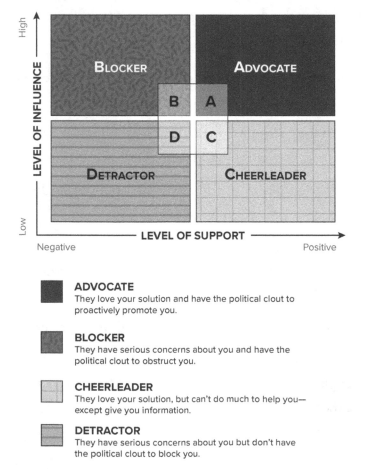

## STAKEHOLDER CATEGORIZATION
A way to analyze stakeholder power and sentiment

**ADVOCATE**
They love your solution and have the political clout to proactively promote you.

**BLOCKER**
They have serious concerns about you and have the political clout to obstruct you.

**CHEERLEADER**
They love your solution, but can't do much to help you—except give you information.

**DETRACTOR**
They have serious concerns about you but don't have the political clout to block you.

Be aware that this is a dynamic mapping exercise. Something may happen to shift a stakeholder's sentiment; therefore, you need to be constantly monitoring this. In fact, your job is to shift stakeholders from the left to the right. In terms of prioritization, your first priority must be addressing your blockers. Think of your blockers as a smoldering fire. Given the right conditions, it can transfer into a catastrophic inferno. Blockers are often very skeptical, and for this reason many sales professionals shy away from them—to their detriment. I've had experiences where some of my most active blockers have flipped to become extremely strong advocates. In my experience it often boils down to them blocking a solution because they don't fully understand how it supports their goals, or they think the vendor is indifferent toward them. After blockers your next priority should be how you can leverage the support of your advocates and cheerleaders. Detractors are important, but you don't have to win over every stakeholder to be successful. You need to win over enough of the right stakeholders, and they will take care of the internal politics.

> *You don't have to win over every stakeholder to be successful. You need to win over enough of the right stakeholders, and they will take care of the internal politics.*

# The Stakeholder Checklist

The following is a checklist we have developed to help you facilitate stakeholder development:

## INFLUENCE

1. Have you validated key goals, objectives, and initiatives?

2. Are you aligning your value and requests for action with stakeholder goals?

3. Have you confirmed each stakeholder's level of influence?

4. Are there any key stakeholders that you have not met?

5. Have you identified or discovered how forces outside the stakeholders' control will jeopardize their key goals and objectives? (market forces, their competitors, etc.)

6. Have you clarified for each stakeholder how the status quo will lead to their misery?

7. Do you understand how their functional role influences their objectives?

8. Do you understand how they are compensated and what KPIs they care about?

## SUPPORT

9. Are you being overly optimistic about stakeholder support? (When in doubt, err on the side of pessimism.)

10. Are the reasons for support or resistance aligned with the stakeholder type? If not, why not?

11. Are all stakeholder types represented in your analysis?

12. How might you leverage the reasons for support to influence other stakeholders?

13. Have you fully leveraged your organization's resources to increase support?

14. Have you shared customer success stories using the hero's journey as an analogy to their situation? Have you created a high-definition vision of the potential pit of despair?

15. How might you reduce or eliminate resistance by aligning your value with the stakeholders' key goals and objectives?

16. What risk might neutral stakeholders present?

## INFLUENCE AND SUPPORT MAP

17. How might you intensify the support of your advocates?

18. How might your inside-outsider take action to advance your position?

19. What strategically relevant information might your inside-outsider provide for you?

20. What urgent action can you take to neutralize or win over blockers?

21. How might you cultivate extreme dissatisfaction with the status quo and/or competing courses of action with blockers and critics?

22. How might you reduce the level of influence of blockers and critics?

23. How might you increase the level of influence and/or support of your cheerleaders?

## POLITICAL MATRIX (THE INTERNAL POLITICS)[14]

24. Which stakeholder(s) present the greatest opportunity for leverage over others? What steps might you take to effectively win their support?

25. How might you optimize the level of support you currently have within the political matrix?

26. Who presents the best opportunity to influence your most influential stakeholder?

27. Have you validated your understanding of the political matrix with your inside-outsider?

## TEAM COVERAGE

28. Have you thought broadly about who might comprise your internal team members (the crew)?

29. Have you aligned your customer's needs with internal stakeholder goals?

30. Have you applied the hero's journey framework to your internal stakeholders?

31. What steps might you and your team members take to improve the quality of relationships with key stakeholders?

32. Are you effectively matching your team members with stakeholders by thinking about functional roles, hierarchical structure, and personality types?

---

14  For a full explanation of the political matrix, check out our course on stakeholder management at http://academy.whetstoneinc.ca.

33. Are you and your team members focusing on creating value and aligning with stakeholder goals in every planned interaction?

34. Are there any lingering issues that might create negative sentiments and embolden your blockers and critics? What steps might you take to reduce or resolve these?

35. Where might a one-on-one meeting be the most effective form of communication?

36. Where might bringing multiple stakeholders and multiple team members together be the most effective?

37. When is it best to use synchronous or asynchronous communication?

38. How might you use virtual communication in a way that is superior to in-person?

39. Have you thought carefully enough about the sequence of actions (at least three steps) required to develop each stakeholder into an inside-outsider?

40. Have you set realistic expectations regarding actions and dates? Have you considered the political landscape?

# Best Practices for Meetings

When meeting with stakeholders, keep in mind the following best practices:

- Have clear behavioral outcomes (e.g., as a result of the meeting, the stakeholder should do something differently).

- Bring value to the stakeholder; don't just pump them for information.

- Change their perspective/beliefs to help them see more clearly.

- Begin and end on time (early if possible).

- Evaluate and leverage the political landscape.

The number of decision makers involved in major corporate purchases has increased in recent years due to the complexity of the buying process and the need for input from multiple departments and stakeholders. This can include individuals from procurement, finance, legal, and the business unit that will be using the product or service. Additionally, the use of cross-functional teams to evaluate potential vendors and make purchasing decisions has become more common. As a result, the decision-making process may involve more people and take longer to complete. Taking the time early in a sales pursuit to understand who these stakeholders are and what they want and need may slow you down in the early part of pursuing a sales opportunity but will accelerate the deal in the later stages.

Whetstone provides training in how to enhance both the crew and the cast. For the purpose of this book, however, we are focusing on the cast to better understand the hero's journey. If you'd like training on stakeholder management, please check out our stakeholder management courses at the Whetstone Academy (http://acadmey.whetstoneinc.ca). If you're a Salesforce user, and you'd like to manage both your external and internal stakeholders directly within Salesforce, check out our Stakeholder Intel app on the AppExchange at www.appexchange.com.

This stakeholder-development checklist is a valuable framework for working with external stakeholders or—as we call them in our movie world—the cast. What I have found during my years of training, however, is that people also need simple guides to shape their thinking, especially in written form. Now it's time to learn how to fill in the critical piece to landing your next engagement—the Hero's Journey: Discovery Storyboard.

# ACT III: APPLICATION

# CHAPTER 7

# THE HERO'S JOURNEY
## DISCOVERY STORYBOARD

*Sometimes the future changes quickly and completely, and we're left with the only choice of what to do next. We can choose to be afraid of it, to stand there trembling, not moving, assuming the worst that can happen, or we can step forward into the unknown and assume it will be brilliant.*
**—Christina Yang, actor**

**A**s I look back over my sales career, what strikes me is the increasing complexity of supplier solutions combined with the increasing complexity of buyer environments and sophistication. I think this is the root cause for the increasing ineffectiveness of sales techniques that are overly prescriptive and complex. As our world becomes more complicated, sales professionals need to rely less on prescribed techniques and more on their ability to think critically. That's where the art and science of storyboarding a professional sale can be so powerful.

Let me give you a bit of background. Storyboarding often forms a crucial part of the preproduction process of film, television, animation, game design, advertising, comics, and book illustration. Developed at Disney Animation Studios in the 1930s, it was first used in a live-action film for *Gone with the Wind*.[15] As film critic Fionnuala Halligan wrote, "The unsung heroes of film, storyboard artists are the first to give vision to a screenplay, translating words on the page into shots for the screen."[16]

*Sales professionals need to rely less on prescribed techniques and more on their ability to think critically.*

Storyboards keep the crew on the same page and are a great way for people working together to visualize their ideas and brainstorm new ones. They guide visual language, scene transitions, action sequences, cinematography, lighting, design, location scouting, costume development, production design, art direction, computer-generated effects, and different phases of animation.

How can we apply this tool to professional sales and account management? When you use the discovery storyboard shown at the beginning of this chapter, you bring people together to determine the characters and the plot. It becomes a document that brings clarity and consensus to the table.

---

15  Ari Chand, "Explainer: What Is Storyboarding for Film?," TheConversation.com, September 23, 2020, https://theconversation.com/explainer-what-is-storyboarding-for-film-131205.

16  Fionnuala Halligan, *The Art of Movie Storyboards* (East Sussex, UK: Ilex Press, 2013).

# THE HERO'S JOURNEY
## DISCOVERY STORYBOARD

Director:_____ Date:_____

Account Name: _____

### ❶ THE HERO
Who is the main decision maker?

### ❷ THE GOAL(S)
What do they want? (long-term, strategic, noble purpose)

### ❸ THE VILLAIN(S)
What external forces are outside of their control and could change their world in ways that will jeopardize their goal achievement?

### ❹ THE FLAW
What weakness(es) exist within the status quo that will be exposed by The Villain(s) and which can be addressed by your solution?

### ❺ THE PIT OF DESPAIR
How will The Hero suffer if no action is taken and The Villain exposes The Flaw?

### ❻ THE SPECIAL RESOURCE
What relevant, special capabilities can you bring that can help The Hero overcome or avoid the misery?

### ❼ THE NEW WORLD
What does the future look like if The Hero works with you?

Let's go through each section of the storyboard to show you how to use it. You do not need to fill it out sequentially. Sometimes, you may have more information on the flaws than the villains. Sometimes, you may start filling it out and realize that you don't have information and need to get it. The main point of the storyboard is that all the sections are important in helping you pursue an opportunity. Think of yourself as Sherlock Holmes. These are the pieces of the puzzle you have to put together.

And the most important point of all? *This is all about story listening.* If you are doing the talking, then you aren't doing the listening that will get you the critical answers to complete your storyboard.

Writing it down in a structured way will clarify your thinking. Who is the hero? What is this story about? What's their goal? Do the rest of the elements tie back to that goal? It will force you to connect the dots in ways that you haven't done before and quickly identify where your thinking may be unclear.

Start by filling in the director. That's you. You are the director of this part of the production as the primary sales lead. Your role is to help both the crew (your internal stakeholders) and the cast (the external stakeholders) have a positive buying experience. You are the director leading the way to support the hero's journey.

# Describing the Hero

*Who is the main decision maker?* Remember, the hero is always a person, not a company. You will be accompanying this hero on their journey, so you want a good understanding of who they are and how they operate. You are focusing on the strategic changemaker, the person who has been allocated that role. It may not be the CEO; the hero may be several levels below the CEO. Who you're selling to has responsibility for executing strategic initiatives aligned with whatever it is you're selling. Ultimately, the people who are feeling the pain (the users) report to the person responsible for strategic goals in the organization (the hero). The hero has the ability to decide which resources they need to acquire in order to achieve the organization's strategic goal.

# Focusing on Goal(s)

*What do they want (long-term, strategic, noble purpose)?* Once you've established the hero, then you want to discover their strategic goal. You want to be careful not to pick a goal that's just convenient to what you happen to sell. For example, if you're doing sales training, it's going to be very easy to say, "The hero wants to improve the competencies of her salespeople, so our goal is to train her sales team." That's just way too convenient.

Instead, focus on their higher, strategic purpose. What's the goal that the customer would continue to pursue even if they never met you and didn't know you existed? Imagine you're a professional speaker and that all you listen for is the fact that a customer's goal is to get a speaker for an upcoming event. You convince the customer that you're the person. You do a wonderful job at the event. Now what? You are back to square one. But what would have happened if you had listened in a different way and came to understand that your customer's goal is to increase market share by 10 percent in the next three years? The event is just a way to rally the troops. Because you listened for the strategic goal, you can come back and say, "You know, here's my understanding of how the industry is changing that could jeopardize your goal. And here are some thoughts I have around how we might work together to increase your probability of success."

Focusing on the goal is often a challenge for salespeople. Historically, we've been trained to look for the pain, and there is a big difference between looking for pain and listening for goals. If you're looking for pain, you're like an aspirin to a headache. "Okay, I need you. I'll take the aspirin or maybe something else. But I just need immediate relief from this headache. Once I've gotten relief, I don't need you anymore."

Goals, especially if they're strategic in nature, are longer term. If you connect at the level of goals, you can build ongoing relationships. Now the customer is thinking, "I want to be healthy in my sixties and seventies. I need a lifestyle coach, supplements, exercise, and stress management. You're providing that. Ten years from now, we'll still be working together."

Additionally, salespeople need to appreciate that our emotions are tied to our goals. The reason we experience emotions is because we are goal oriented. If you're a golfer, you know the distress you feel when you're putting for a birdie and end up with a bogey. If you're not a golfer, think of your favorite spectator sport and how you felt when your team, in a high-stakes game, was on the verge of victory but ended up losing. Anything that facilitates or supports our goals makes us feel good. Anything that jeopardizes our goals makes us feel bad. If you feel bad, you're going to avoid something. If you feel good, you're going to approach it. This all happens on the subconscious level.

## Understanding the Villain(s)

*What external forces are outside of their control and could change their world in ways that will jeopardize their goal achievement?* Suppose the villain is skyrocketing energy costs. Whatever you're selling, do deep-dive research to understand the potential implications of those rising energy costs on the customer so you can bring this to the hero's attention. Understanding the villain is the quickest way to get appointments with senior executives, because they also need a clear understanding of the world around them and how it's changing. Share with them your insights and ideas about how they can navigate this new world. It's an extremely powerful way for salespeople to gain access to senior executives.

A good analysis tool to help you understand external forces that might impact your customer is PESTLE. PESTLE analysis is a framework used to analyze the external factors that may have an impact on an organization. The initialism stands for

**Political**: This looks at the impact of government policies, political stability, and the legal environment on the organization.

**Economic**: This examines the impact of the broader economic environment on the organization, including factors such as inflation, interest rates, and the overall state of the economy.

**Sociocultural**: This looks at the impact of cultural and social factors on the organization, including demographic trends, consumer attitudes, and values.

**Technological**: This considers the impact of advances in technology on the organization, including new products and services, automation, and the internet.

**Legal**: This looks at the impact of laws, regulations, and legal issues on the organization.

**Environmental**: This examines the impact of the physical environment, including factors such as weather patterns, natural disasters, and climate change, on the organization.

The PESTLE analysis is often used as a starting point for a strategic analysis of an organization, providing a holistic view of the external factors that may affect it. By understanding and articulating these factors, you can help your customer anticipate changes in their environment. Here are some questions to get you started:

- What is the political situation of the country, and how can it affect the industry?

- What are the prevalent economic factors?

- How much importance does culture have in the market, and what are its determinants?

- What technological innovations are likely to pop up and affect the market structure?

- Are there any current legislations that regulate the industry, or can there be any change in the legislations for the industry?

- What are the environmental concerns for the industry?[17]

One of the ways you might consider presenting potential villains using PESTLE is by using a radar or spider graph. In this graph, the closer a force is to the middle, the more your customer should pay attention to it. You can then discuss the details of the most important factors. In the following example, technology, economic, and environmental forces are more threatening than political, legal, and social forces. This visual representation can help bring villains to life.

---

17    PESTLE Analysis, "What Is PESTLE Analysis? An Important Business Analysis Tool," PESTLEAnalysis.com, accessed February 8, 2023, https://pestleanalysis.com/what-is-pestle-analysis/.

## PESTLE
### External Factors Affecting My Customer

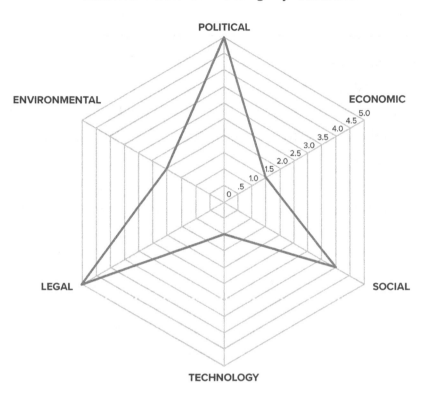

Understanding the villain is directly tied to being relevant to the customer. Most executives are so preoccupied with the challenges inside their company and against their competition that they may not notice how the world around them is changing. Often, sales professionals are interested in explaining *what they sell*, especially if it's a robust and comprehensive solution. They feel the need to educate the customer on their solution and can't wait to talk about it. What they find hard to believe is that their solution is irrelevant to the customer. Just because it's a wonderful solution doesn't make it relevant. The more senior the executives, the more we have to establish that immediate sense of relevance.

One of the ways we can do this is with the villain. Rather than starting with your product or solution, demonstrate expertise in the industry you're selling into and the external forces that are acting on the industry players, especially if those forces are changing or emerging. That's what's going to get someone's attention. Think of a wild animal in the forest. The minute it hears footsteps, it panics because its environment is changing, and that could represent a threat. That's the way the brain is wired. That's why when you speak with a degree of expertise and competence about industry forces, you're absolutely going to get the attention of business executives.

The villain must be outside of the hero's control. It cannot be something that the hero believes wouldn't happen to them because they wouldn't act that way. It needs to be something that could happen to anybody and is not their fault. Sometimes, salespeople get confused between the villain and the flaw. They take things that the hero can fix and try to make that the villain. I always stop them by saying, "Your customer is probably thinking, 'I would never be so stupid. I would fix that.' So make sure the villain is outside their control and is ultimately leading to the thing that you need them to fix—that's the flaw."

## Discovering the Flaw

*What weakness(es) exist(s) within the status quo that will be exposed by the villain(s), and which can be addressed by your solution?* The flaw is what is within the hero's control. Often, the flaw is felt first by the user community. The user community is where you'll find an inside-outsider who can show you what is going wrong. That inside-outsider knows that when things start going south inside the organization, there are consequences. Maybe, there's more waste than there used to be. Or the company is not able to get product out in time. Or the product doesn't have the right quality. Customers are beginning to complain.

The flaw is usually a business process and/or infrastructure that has become part of the status quo. Invisible in nature, it may have been something that worked before but is not working now. The flaw is so ingrained in the process that when the world changes, it's hard to see. It's below the surface, often a belief system that holds the current infrastructure and processes in place.

The flaw is where salespeople live. They've been trained to find the pain and then offer aspirin. The problem is their aspirin is commoditized, because everybody has aspirin or the equivalent. When they find the pain, they are surprised that the company they're selling to postpones, procrastinates, or decides not to address the pain. The salesperson ends up perplexed: "I see this pain so clearly. Why won't you address it?" The answer is simple. They have other priorities. Every single business we sell to has pain they do not address and have decided to live with. This is very frustrating to salespeople.

I'm not saying not to find the pain. I am recommending that you prioritize the pain by having a fuller context. You need the bigger story so that when the users go to the economic stakeholder for approval, the economic stakeholder understands that it is strategically important.

This is where the inside-outsider plays a major role. They realize that if the organization continues to do things the way it's always done, then it's going to get in big trouble. They become the point of access.

As a salesperson, however, you need to be careful that once you find the inside-outsider and define the pain, you do not go straight to the solution. Slow down. You need to be clear on the pit of despair. How exactly will they suffer if they do nothing?

# Describing the Pit of Despair

*How will the hero suffer if no action is taken and the villain exposes the flaw?* I am going to spend extra time on this idea, since it is the one that many salespeople struggle with. They are able to grasp that they are not the hero; the villain is external forces; the flaw is internal systems and culture; and the focus of the special resource is to help bring the hero into a new world of transformation. But the pit of despair and what to do with it can seem almost counterintuitive to many sales teams.

The pit of despair is the antidote to status quo bias. Status quo bias is the subconscious preference that everybody in the organization has to leave things just the way they are. Whatever proposal you put in front of an organization, you're taking it into the unfamiliar. While you are updating your CRM to an 80 percent probability of closure, your customer is hitting status quo bias inside the organization and even within themselves. They begin to second-guess or reconsider the decision they're making because the pain of staying the same is less than their perceived pain of change.

You need to fully understand the pit of despair and convey that to your customer. They will want to do nothing, but you need to create clarity around the consequences of doing nothing. The pit of despair does not have to be actual suffering. It's just as powerful when it is anticipated suffering. Just think of the power of a movie like *Jaws* where the anticipation of the shark getting you is as scary as the actual attack. Salespeople sometimes don't understand anticipated suffering can be just as worrisome as actual suffering and maybe even more so.

The pit of despair is what happens in science fiction movies. In *The Avengers,* everything goes wrong. Every hero is in a fight for their life until all of a sudden, somebody comes in to save the day. The pit of despair also forces introspection. Think *Ironman*. When the hero is in the ordinary world pursuing their goal and everything's working well, they're overconfident, arrogant, and often complacent. If you're trying to sell to somebody who's in the ordinary world, and everything's going well, they won't give you the time of day. They don't see why you're necessary. *The pit of despair humbles the hero.*

The hero has a way of doing things that works for them. They wash, rinse, and repeat. When an inciting incident occurs that pushes them into a world of chaos, nothing works. In fact, the more the hero applies their proven success formula, the worse it gets. They don't know how to navigate out of the pit of despair.

The pandemic is a great example. Nobody could change what was happening or the resulting economic global lockdown. But businesses still needed to sell to their customers. Instead of feeling helpless and complaining about the pandemic, they had to look at their infrastructure and make sure their salespeople had good laptops and cameras, because the status quo became detrimental. They had to overcome weaknesses in order to navigate in a new world.

Let's take a look at the suspense-thriller, *The Invisible Guest*. A businessman wakes up in a locked hotel room next to a dead body. When he is accused of murder, he hires a lawyer, and they work through the night to find out what happened. The protagonist is bewildered by the misery he is in, and the lawyer (the special resource) says to him, "There is no salvation without suffering." I love that line. She's telling him that if he wants to come out of this, he needs to accept the suffering that has befallen him. Don't try to avoid it. We have to go through the fire because that's what shapes us. This means the pit of despair is not all bad. In fact, it's a critical part of the hero's transformation. Without it the hero would not grow. Suffering is good for the capable and competent people that we sell to. It slows them down. It causes them to think, rethink, and be open to intervention.

Let me take you through a simple dialogue with a group of salespeople I worked with relating to the pit of despair. This group didn't appreciate how important it is to counteract status quo bias. They were intent on avoiding the pit of despair when talking with the customer.

| | |
|---|---|
| Salesperson: | "They're going to lose market share." |
| Me: | "Okay, so what?" |
| Salesperson: | "They'll lose market share in other geographies as well." |
| Me: | "Okay, so what?" |
| Salesperson: | "Their revenue will drop." |
| Me: | "Okay, so what?" |
| Salesperson: | "Their reputation will be damaged." |
| Me: | "Okay, so what?" |
| Salesperson: | "They could lose their business." |

Bingo! That's it! We had to work with him to help him take it down to the level of catastrophe. And here is where almost all sales professionals make a fatal mistake. This salesperson avoided the pit because it's unpleasant to think about. We're all inclined to act this way. Why? Because we're problem solvers. We want to help. We're optimists. Even in our own careers, if we lose a big sale, it's okay because there's another one out there. We're naturally optimistic. We want to help others. We want to make people feel good, and we want them to like us. As soon as we see any hint of trouble, we immediately react with, "Oh, we've got a solution for that." We relieve the tension.

*We need to do the opposite.* Instead of offering a solution, we need to allow the hero to experience the pit of despair. We need to allow the tension to grow. But remember, time is not your friend. The more people live with pain, the more they're able to live with pain. I know people with tremendous migraines or back pain who have just learned to cope. Businesses are like that as well. They learn to tolerate pain. That's why it's important to activate that sense of urgency.

> *Instead of offering a solution, we need to allow the hero to experience the pit of despair. We need to allow the tension to grow.*

Emotions—scared, mad, and sad—drive urgency because they are tied to survival. Emotions like desire, which are tied to being glad, drive loyalty. Glad works if we are working together for that five-year goal. That's how you create loyalty. But you have to create urgency and a separation from the status quo to land a customer.

I want to end this discussion of the pit of despair with one more thought. Neuroscientist David Rock, the cofounder and CEO of NeuroLeadership Institute, has a model about how electrical chemical activity in the brain is based on threats and rewards. The brain works to avoid physical threats and to pursue rewards. For example, I was walking in London a few years ago at night in an unfamiliar section. An explosion went off, and I had this out-of-body experience observing myself. I completely froze except for my head, which automatically turned toward the source of the noise. Within a split second, I figured out it was fireworks and felt a wave of relief come over my body. My paralysis ended, and I continued walking.

Dr. Rock says human beings react in the same way to social threats (e.g., demotion) and social rewards (e.g., promotion) as they do to physical ones. In fact, most of the threats we face today are social. He created the SCARF model that involves five domains of human social experience: status, certainty, autonomy, relatedness, and fairness.[18]

As you engage customers, your words matter. As you speak they will automatically and subconsciously process what you're saying through these five lenses. Your words are either driving them into the pit of despair or to the summit of victory in the new world. Status is tied to *survival*. Anything that enhances or threatens status will cause the brain to release chemicals that create feelings of stress and anxiety or feelings of euphoria and relief. Greater status increases the probability of survival and fulfillment, as people of higher status have better access to important resources. The brain loves *certainty* and hates what's unfamiliar. The brain struggles to keep us alive in environments where it can't be sure what will happen next. This causes stress. Conversely, being clear about what will happen next creates relief. We always want *autonomy*. Autonomy means we have freedom of choice. When our brain feels like all options are open to us, we have a greater sense of fulfillment, as we believe we'll be able to take the necessary course of action to stay alive and be fulfilled. Anytime we feel our freedom has been restricted, we react negatively. *Relatedness* means we are fundamentally tribal and want a sense of belonging. We don't want to be alienated from our tribe. Any situations that unfold, such as a promotion or relocation, where we envision we'll be cut off from our established network, will produce anxiety.

---

18   Acronymat, "SCARF," Acronymat.com, accessed February 8, 2023, https://www. acronymat.com/2022/05/25/scarf/.

# BE A BETTER LEADER WITH SCARF

SCARF represents five areas influencing human behavior. The human brain wants to minimize danger or maximize reward which activate respective responses. It explains and helps to deal with human reactions, motivations, and interactions.

| | | REWARD STATE ACTIVATORS | THREAT STATE ACTIVATORS |
|---|---|---|---|
| **S** | **STATUS** Relative importance to others, personal worth | Positive and mutual feedback, public acknowledgment | Critique, unsolicited advice |
| **C** | **CERTAINTY** Ability to predict the future | Clear goals and expectations, feasible schedules | Non-transparent, dishonest and unpredictable behavior |
| **A** | **AUTONOMY** Sense of control over events | Providing choices, empowerment, self-responsibility, self-organization | Micromanagement, command and control |
| **R** | **RELATEDNESS** Feeling safe around others | Mentoring, enabling socializations | Internal competition, prohibition of socializing |
| **F** | **FAIRNESS** Perception of people interactions fairness | Transparent decisions and communication, clear rules | Unequal conditions, lack of rules and communication |

Finally, we have a deeply ingrained need to be treated with *fairness* and to see others that we love being treated fairly. We experience moral outrage if we are not treated fairly. *Marriage Story* is a great example of fairness. The movie explores the complexity and dysfunction of divorce, and we witness firsthand the wide range of emotions experienced by both parties and how each feels treated unfairly. The devastation that follows is as unavoidable as it is unfortunate.

The SCARF model works in analyzing the pit of despair by highlighting the impact of social threats. It is also helpful in thinking and talking about the new world, because transformation potentially promises greater status, certainty, autonomy, relatedness, and fairness.

# Designing the Special Resource

*What relevant, special capabilities can you bring that can help the hero overcome or avoid the misery?* For sales professionals, this is the heart of the matter. This is where we bring value. Everything else in this book is context for the potential value we can bring to our customers. The special resource is the relevant and tailored resources you are going to bring to the table to help the hero out of the pit of despair. The two key words in this definition are "relevant" and "tailored." Think in terms of movies. All romantic comedies are formulaic, but if they are not interesting or relevant, you will experience a big yawn. If the special resource is just following a formula, you will have a disconnect.

I recently started working with a company that has a breakthrough solution with real value. When I listened to the salespeople, all I heard was a canned pitch. Sometimes, they didn't even go through the discovery process before meeting with the decision maker. The salespeople presented their solution as if it were going to set the world on fire. They ended up in meetings concluding with the kiss of death: "We'll think about it and get back to you." If the sales team listened more carefully and spoke more specifically, they could have shown their customers how they can actually help in a particular situation. The salespeople would have said a lot less, but with a lot more meaning. And they'd be in a much stronger position to show how their particular special resource has been tailored to the customer's specific situation.

Sometimes it can be really frustrating when you have a revolutionary solution, but you encounter resistance. You try to dig deeper, but you just can't understand what is holding your customer back. One of my clients is an executive at a large pharmaceutical company. He trains his team not only to go deeper to understand a customer's resistance, but to go across. Through experience he has learned that there are only five reasons for customer resistance, which he summarizes with the acronym FT-NUT:

1. Finance—they don't have the budget.

2. Time—they can't find the time.

3. Need—it's not addressing what they really need.

4. Urgency—it's not a priority at this time.

5. Trust—you lack credibility.

He recounts how using this framework enabled him to get to the real reason for resistance in a particular situation. The potential customer began with a concern about their product being too expensive. This was rather shocking because of the breakthrough nature of the solution and how it could revolutionize how the doctor could care for his patients. Rather than just going deeper on the budget issue, he went across and uncovered the real issue was trust. As they talked, the doctor revealed that he had concerns about their research and how the patients were selected for the clinical trials. The resistance wasn't about budget; it was about trust. Once that was properly addressed, the doctor's comfort level to move forward rose.

One final point about the special resource. Things will always go wrong, and that's okay. It's not surprising or unexpected. It's part of the story. In fact, if you tell people that you're going to wave a magic wand and everything's going to be perfect, they won't believe you. The hero has to struggle and fight to get out of the pit of despair. The special resource is there to help. Nobody expects a smooth ride, but the hero will come through it, be proud of what they've done, and want other people to know about the successful intervention.

I remember one training program we did where there was limited uptake. In fact, the participants appeared indifferent. The leader knew his people and what they needed and other internal issues they were grappling with. He said they were going to work through it. He made some internal changes to help the participants understand how this training fit in with other training they recently received. Once the sales team had the proper context, engagement jumped, and my client saw great results.

## The New World

*What does the future look like if the hero works with you?* The new world is a result of your intervention. The new world addresses the question, how does the hero win and become transformed?

Imagine a company is trying to grow market share in a particular country. Everything looks great until suddenly the government imposes several unfavorable regulatory changes. Profitability plummets. Do they need to close stores and lay off people? How will their investors react? Then a supplier comes along with equipment that addresses the new regulations while reducing costs and increasing productivity. That's the special resource. It's going to be a struggle to replace the equipment, but if they implement the solution, they will emerge into a new world with new capabilities. They will have transformed their business. Maybe they will not only realize the benefits promised by the new supplier, but also provide a whole new customer experience. The company is capable of a lot more going forward.

Once you have completed the Hero's Journey: Discovery Storyboard, you are ready to hook into the hero emotionally by telling them a success story. This form is structured and has a specific order in which to tell a story. Like the other tools in this book, it has been used with thousands of professional salespeople with significant success.

CHAPTER 8

# THE HERO'S JOURNEY
## SUCCESS STORYBOARD

*The hero's journey always begins with the call. One way or another, a guide must come to speak to us of a plan for the universe that we will be at the center of.*
**—Joseph Campbell, author**

Ninety-five percent of salespeople understand the power of storytelling. In fact, the best salespeople intuitively tell stories. My observation, however, is that they tell stories about organizations instead of people. It's almost like they're afraid to speak about people. That's where their stories fall short. To elicit emotion and empathy, you have to talk at the level of the person, the human being. We don't feel empathy for buildings, concepts, or organizations. And if you don't elicit emotion or empathy, you will be challenged to make a sale.

I find that the stories of many professional salespeople sound too intellectual or are focused on engaging critical thinking from the customer. The salesperson talks about organizations, as opposed to talking about the people in those organizations—people just like you and me. When we tell stories about people, listeners appreciate the emotion of what's happening and think, "Wow, that could happen to me." Without a doubt, storytelling is much more impactful at a personal level, yet most salespeople act as if it is almost unprofessional to talk that way and want to keep stories at a business-case level.

They forget about the power of emotions. Dr. Alan Watkins, neuroscientist, CEO and cofounder of Complete, an organization dedicated to developing emotionally intelligent leaders, has so far identified thirty-four thousand human emotions. In their mobile app, Universe of Emotions, they have categorized two thousand of these thirty-four thousand emotions. The app clusters emotions that are adjacent to each other, and while it's a step toward simplifying the neuroscience of emotion, two thousand emotions are still a lot to digest. Salespeople need to be emotionally intelligent, but not that intelligent. We can't spend all day trying to understand all those different emotions. But we do need to use them. Remember my example of the movie *Elvis*. It's two hours and forty minutes long. The reason we sit through this movie without balking at the length is because the story is told in a way that keeps us emotionally glued.

*When you have a meaningful and lofty goal, there will be a struggle to achieve it.*

Actually, all emotions can be boiled down to four primary ones—scared, mad, sad, or glad.[19] You may have noticed that three out of four of these primary emotions are negative. Well, life is not easy. That's why the most compelling stories emphasize negative emotions. When you have a

---

19   Julie Beck, "New Research Says There Are Only Four Emotions," *The Atlantic*, February 4, 2014, https://www.theatlantic.com/health/archive/2014/02/new-research-says-there-are-only-four-emotions/283560/.

meaningful and lofty goal, there will be a struggle to achieve it. It will be difficult to leave the status quo. To paraphrase Aristotle: if there's no struggle, then there's no story. There can only be a struggle if there are goals, which means we understand what our customer is really trying to achieve.

Let me tell you a story about how emotions played into getting a sale. A systems integration partner wanted to get us into a company they worked for that was making a major investment in a billing system. They wanted us to get the business because for every dollar we sold, they would sell five dollars in services. After a bit of legwork, I finally reached the CIO and quickly introduced myself. He abruptly interrupted and said, "I am not at all interested." Then he hung up the phone on me. I was absolutely stunned. This had never happened. I tried to get back in touch with him, but he would not take my calls.

Since I had nothing to lose, I worked to get in front of the CEO. She actually took my call, and I explained that we were the number-one supplier in this space, but nobody from her company has spoken to us even though they were making a mission-critical investment. I asked for half an hour to share what we did and why so many of her peers were investing in our platform.

We got our meeting and asked great strategic questions. When they finished sharing with me, I told them a story about what we were doing for one of their counterparts, which was a sister company in the United States. It took less than two minutes, but I knew magic had happened. Within two weeks the CIO was fired. In two more weeks, we signed a $4 million software agreement with another $20 million in services. Everything changed with that one story I told.

Telling a success story is an art like being a screenwriter. The screenwriter starts with a blank scene. Their job is to creatively paint a picture that activates the imagination. You are activating the imagination of the customer. Every word triggers their imagination.

A note of caution: many sales professionals that I train can't resist the urge to come out of their story in the midst of it in order to editorialize. This is a big mistake, as it breaks the spell of the story. An epic example of just letting the hero's experience speak for itself is the story of the Jewish pianist Wladyslaw Szpilman during the Holocaust. His autobiography was brought to the big screen in the movie *The Piano*. What is remarkable about this storytelling is there is no editorializing. Events unfold before us through the eyes of Szpilman. We simply experience the highs and lows with him without the storyteller telling us what we should think or feel. We experience the story as if it were our own. That's what you should aim for. Let the story do the work. Just tell it.

Too often salespeople forget to have fun with the story. They think every word must be precise and professional. My advice is to get out of your professional role. I ask the people I train to tell stories as if they were sitting around the dinner table with family or friends. Soon they're telling them like there's no tomorrow. It becomes natural because this is what we've been doing all of our lives—hearing and sharing stories. When you relax, you can put your own personality into your stories. The art of storytelling comes from being comfortable in your own skin and marrying your personality with the storytelling.

Storytelling is also a science. The science is the structure like the one I am going to show you. It reminds me of a very skilled pianist. She is all about structure because she knows that creativity happens on top of structure. First, you learn the scales and discipline yourself. The more you do that, the more creative and sophisticated you become. But first you need to lay the foundation.

# THE HERO'S JOURNEY
## SUCCESS STORYBOARD

Director:_____ Date:_____

Account Name: _____

## ACT 1

1️⃣ What you've shared reminds me of (existing customer name)

2️⃣ Like you (existing customer role)

3️⃣ And like you (existing customer goal)

## ACT 2

1️⃣ Unfortunately ( sudden adversarial change)

2️⃣ Worried because (existing customer's pit of despair)

3️⃣ (Existing customer) realized (flaw)

4️⃣ Fortunately (how you came into the hero's movie)

5️⃣ We worked together to introduce joint solution

## ACT 3

1️⃣ As a result (existing customer) was able to (describe what they were able to fix)

2️⃣ And now (describe the new world)

Let's build that foundation using the Hero's Journey: Success Storyboard template. Think of it as the building blocks you need to elicit emotion. How you tell the story will be based on your personality, but you need to nail the structure, and this happens through a strong foundation.

I have divided this form into three "scenes" just like a movie.

- Scene one sets up relevancy between you and the hero in your success story.

- Scene two talks about the problem and how you as the director helped the hero solve it.

- Scene three talks about the results and the new world.

You're going to fill in the answers to ten statements. The order is very important, as are clarity and succinctness. As you can see, the story you are telling is the hero's journey. You want to tell this story in less than two minutes. This is what the sequence looks like:

1. What you've shared reminds me of *(existing customer name)*

2. Like you *(existing customer role)*

3. And like you *(existing customer goal)*

4. Unfortunately *(sudden adversarial change)*

5. Worried because *(existing customer's pit of despair)*

6. *(Existing customer)* realized *(flaw)*

7. Fortunately *(how you came into the hero's movie)*

8. We worked together to introduce *(joint solution)*

9. As a result *(existing customer)* was able to *(describe what they were able to fix)*

10. And now *(describe the new world)*

# The Importance of Relevancy

When you tell a story, you are choosing one that has relevance and creates a sympathetic hero. Forrest Gump is a great example of a sympathetic hero, portrayed so well by Tom Hanks that when he falls into despair, many viewers have burst into tears. That's good storytelling! Get your audience to connect with and sympathize with your hero, then take your hero on a journey, knowing after successfully connecting the audience to your hero, they will feel what the hero feels.

In your success story, your hero has to be someone your customer connects with. It doesn't have to exactly match your discovery storyboard, but it needs to be similar. The hero needs to be pursuing a similar goal. The most important phrase is "like you." You need to select a story where the person in the success story has a similar role to your customer. Your customer needs to be able to relate to them emotionally. What is critical is that this story is about the hero you helped, not about what you did. It is the hero's success story. The minute the salesperson introduces themselves too early or introduces themselves as the hero, they break the spell.

Relevancy is always about role and goal. Maybe you're talking to a VP of sales and the story you tell is about a director of sales. You need to talk about them as a sales leader who is leading a team. As a sales leader, you need to hit quota, build your people, and create a great culture. Your story aligns with their goals.

Stories impact us because they interrupt the story we are currently telling ourselves about ourselves. While we listen to someone else's story, this allows us to experience someone else's reality and compare it to our own. I'll never forget a scene in the movie *Chicken Run*. Mrs. Tweedy, the chicken farmer's wife, is frustrated because the farm isn't doing well. While she's sorting through the day's mail of mostly overdue invoices, she blurts out, "I'm sick and tired of making minuscule profits!" She opens the next piece of mail and reads, "Are you sick and tired of making minuscule profits?" Of course she's intrigued and acts on the offer. Our stories must meet our customer where they are and then take them from there to their new world if they act on our offer.

Remember your story should take less than two minutes to tell because you are keeping it at a high level, so they remain captivated. You also need to get permission to tell the story. Your expectation should be that if your prospect knows a person you are referencing, they will connect with them for a more detailed version. If they don't know the person you are referencing, they may ask you if they can talk with them. You need to be able to say yes.

When I am training salespeople on storytelling, I inevitably get this comment: "I work in a very small industry, and people are going to know who I'm talking about if I say the name. I'm uncomfortable with that." There's a way to avoid this issue by how you frame the beginning of the story. "What you shared reminds me of George—not his real name, but he has given me permission to tell the story." By the middle of the story, there's a strong possibility your prospect would have forgotten the hero's name. They don't care. They care about themselves. The person in the story opens the door for them to come into the story and assume that person's identity.

Whether someone is a CEO, COO, CFO, or CTO, individual roles tend to have a handful of goals across industries. A head of sales needs to grow sales, develop people, and improve profitability. An operations leader has to increase efficiency and effectiveness. Whoever you're selling to understands the two or three things that somebody in their role is going to be concerned about. Find a customer that you've helped make successful in a way that addresses those two or three goals. Have their story in your back pocket and, based on whatever goal the prospect shares with you, you should be able to take it up pretty quickly to the right level—improving profitability, increasing market share, improving efficiency, lowering waste, and so forth.

There are other variables to help you determine the relevancy of your story. Back in the late 1990s when I came back from California with my thirty stories, I would look at the size of the company, the geographic location, and the industry to try to figure out which of my stories would be relevant. Sometimes, I did not have a story that was relevant to my prospect's industry, but I quickly learned that what matters more than industry is role and goal.

This is how it would play out. "John, you know you remind me of Dom White, who's also a chief operating officer and was also trying to increase efficiency." The nuance that Dom was in pharmaceuticals and John is in manufacturing becomes irrelevant. The minute I say, "Hey, you remind me of same role, same goal," the primitive part of the brain wakes up, especially if that goal is suddenly jeopardized. Vicariously, your customers begin to live through the story. This is how the brain experiments with alternate realities in order to help us better navigate life's uncertainties.

Recently, I watched a movie called *Boiling Point*. It's about this top chef in the UK whose life is crashing from the pressure. I'm not a chef. I'll never be a chef. I can hardly function in a kitchen. But I could relate to him because of the fact that this is a human being who wants something, and what he wants is being jeopardized. I was totally immersed in the movie. There's a part of us that wants to empathize, understand, and connect with others. It does not have to be a perfect match. Even if I don't see a middle-aged Black man like me on the screen, I am still interested in watching the movie and am living vicariously in the story. I came out of *Boiling Point* with a greater sense of empathy and understanding of what happens behind the scenes in a restaurant. In fact, this is how our world changes. It's when a man is immersed in a story about how a woman suffers when she doesn't have the ability to vote. It's when an American watches a movie about a Japanese man wrongfully held in an internment camp. Remember what Stalin said: The death of millions is a statistic. The death of one is a tragedy. It is the power of the storyteller to connect to the emotionally compelling story of one individual that changes whole societies. This must be why Plato said it is the storytellers who rule society.

Another variable in relevancy is accessibility. As I mentioned earlier, I have a customer who I helped win a $2 billion deal. He was laser focused on the hero's journey and happy to give me credit for my role. It's a phenomenal success story for Whetstone, but I can't tell it to a lot of prospects because it's so far out of anything they'll ever deal with. It's just not relevant to them. I'd rather tell the story of somebody who won a $30 million deal or a $3 million deal because they're more accessible.

## Keep the Plotline Moving

The purpose of a success story is to elicit emotion, not give information. I always have to emphasize this in training. In fact, in telling a great success story, our purpose is to *withhold information* and all that great stuff you did for the customer. We don't want to talk about that; we want to use the story to make people have an appetite to learn about those things.

The purpose of the story is about the emotion of connectedness, relating, and empathy for the hero. It's having the prospect say, "I like this person. I can relate to them." Then you build the emotions of fear and anxiety—fear about the uncertainty, followed by the anxiety that comes from sudden, unexpected, or adversarial change. This is followed in the plotline by the realization that if we just turn up the dial, it could allow us to get out of this—a sense of empowerment that it can be fixed.

## Clarity in Storytelling

Clarity is critical because if you confuse me, I'll disengage. There needs to be this very clear plotline through the story for me to follow and not have the interference of "Wait a minute, I thought you said this, and I'm lost now." If that happens, it's fatal. Remember, the brain is obsessed with cause and effect. That's what it lives for. The more cause-and-effect relationships the brain understands, the better job it can do of predicting what's going to happen next. When we are telling our story, the listener's brain is looking for causes. The minute you create fuzziness or lack of clarity with cause and effect, you've lost them.

## Rehearsing and Gathering Stories

I love the saying that "your stories walk the halls after you do." That's such a powerful thought. You go in, drop a story, and leave. That story starts to circulate within the organization. And remember, the story you tell doesn't need to be your story. You're passing on the information. Your company is the special resource, and the story can be used to benefit any salesperson in your organization. These stories are critical company assets, especially in an age of skepticism and inattention.

I encourage sales teams to have "lunch-and-learn events" where they share success stories. One week a rep shares a story. The ten people listening now have a story they can add to their list. Next week it's your turn. Now another salesperson listens to your story and can add it to their list. Often, sales reps only need to hear a story once, and they're able to repeat it. All the stories that I took back from Silicon Valley I only heard once and could repeat them. That's the way stories are. If they're simple and clear, people see it in their mind's eye.

## Storytelling in a Virtual World

Can you tell your story effectively on Zoom or in an email? Absolutely. What's always true is that human beings are interested in other human beings. We are particularly interested in stories of other humans. Clearly, stories predate Zoom, but stories also predate the dinner table and even the campfire. It doesn't matter what the technological platform is that we find ourselves using to share stories. The reality is human beings have always shared stories with each other. That's what we do.

Given the challenges of the virtual world, I think there is an even greater need to tell stories, because storytelling is one of the ways we can overcome virtual meeting challenges and level the playing field. I can have an audience of one or one thousand. It's my storytelling that's going to capture attention. The virtual world of professional selling is not going away, and it's a significant opportunity to differentiate ourselves from the competition by bringing storytelling into our conversations.

*Storytelling is one of the ways we can overcome virtual meeting challenges and level the playing field.*

While you can tell stories on the phone, it is more effective when cameras are on so you can more accurately gauge the level of interest. When the camera is on, make sure you are framed properly and making good eye contact. Email storytelling is an option, but I am a big proponent of live storytelling because the prospect is keeping eye contact with me. I like to see their reactions in real time.

# Adjusting a Success Story to Multiple Audiences

When you help a customer to be successful, many people benefit from that success. I've been working with a company for more than ten years, and they have been extremely successful. Their story is terrific, and when I tell it, I adjust the perspective depending on who I'm talking to. If I'm talking to a chief executive of a midsize firm, this story is always relevant because this is a chief executive trying to grow her business while facing insurmountable odds. Her partner, who's also part owner, is the head of sales. When talking to a sales leader, I tell the same story, but this time it's from the perspective of the head of sales. They have two salespeople who began the training ten years ago and are now directors of strategic accounts. If I'm talking to a salesperson, I tell the story from one of these two perspectives. If I'm talking to an HR person, I tell the story from a talent-development perspective.

When you create success for a customer, go back to that customer and get the story from different perspectives. Yes, there's one main character to the big story. But within that big story, there are little stories. Within those little stories, there are relatable heroes. The main point I want to emphasize is don't take your success for granted. It's multidimensional. Because the pain is multidimensional, the success that resolves that pain is also multidimensional.

# Story Use in Strategic Account Management

The story structure I have described in this chapter is primarily used as a sales tool. Stories, however, are also effective in account management. I do workshops for chief executives multiple times per quarter. They are less interested in sales, but they like the archetype of the hero's journey. They see it as a great tool to develop their most important customers. Many times they realize that they can grow their sales more effectively by focusing on the accounts they already have rather than always hunting for new logos. They also take the framework and apply it to their people to help them get through change and keep them inspired. The hero's journey is a great sales, account management, and leadership tool.

Through your skillful use of the Hero's Journey: Discovery Storyboard and the Hero's Journey: Success Storyboard, you have taken your customer through a winning buying experience. You are not done yet. It's time to take this production out to location. That takes a bit of planning. I have one last tool to share with you—the Hero's Journey: Action Storyboard.

# CHAPTER 9

# THE HERO'S JOURNEY

## ACTION STORYBOARD

*The hero's journey is not just about the adventure, it's about the transformation.*
**—Tom Hiddleston, actor**

The Hero's Journey: Action Plan is the skeletal framework of the project plan. One of the reasons to fill out this form when you are confident that the contract is going to be signed is that it moves you into the "making" mindset without a serious investment of time and money. Often in professional sales there is a time lag between the yes and the legal signing of contracts. It's easy to lose momentum without a document that begins to frame out the project.

This simple form keeps you thinking and keeps the crew and the cast engaged until the big kickoff. The form can also become the first shared "work" document between your organization and the new customer. It's valuable as a quick summary to transition between sales and account management.

# THE HERO'S JOURNEY
## ACTION STORYBOARD

Director:_____ Hero: _____

Executive Producer: _____

Project Status: _____ Budget: _____

| STRATEGIC GOAL: | |
| --- | --- |
| **NOTES:** | |
| **CREW:** | **CAST:** |
| **CURRENT SCENE** | **DESIRED SCENE (OUTCOME):** |
| **KICKOFF** | |
| **POTENTIAL OBSTACLES:** | **LEADING INDICATORS:** |
| **PRODUCTION SCHEDULE (KEY MILESTONES):** | |

The top of the form states who is the director and the hero. Sometimes, depending on the company and the significance of the customer, the director at this stage moves from sales to a strategic account manager or a customer service manager. Clearly, identifying the hero sets the tone of the engagement for everyone.

The executive producer is also named to ensure that proper resources are allocated to the director and crew. Additional information includes the project status and budget. The budget amount should be taken directly from the approved proposal.

Starting off with the strategic goal lets everyone know exactly what the project will be measured against in terms of success. This strategic goal should be as specific as possible for measurement purposes.

The current scene is a brief summary of the status quo, while the desired scene focuses on the desired outcome that will enable the achievement of the strategic goal. Again, this is written to establish clarity during the launch of the project.

Even though at this point in the project personnel decisions may still be underway, it is valuable to outline the major cast members (external resources) and crew members (internal resources) that will be essential to the success of the project. This can be taken directly from the proposal. Instead of names, roles can be listed.

Next, capture the capabilities and resources that will be used to successfully complete the project. What is the full range of solutions you'll be bringing to the customer? And since this is a joint document between your company and the customer, include the top capabilities and resources from both organizations.

The kickoff plan outlines the next-step strategy to launch the project. This can include everything ranging from communications and resource gathering to setting up or incorporating systems. For the potential obstacles section, list any potential barriers to success.

Listing them up front keeps communication transparent from the beginning.

Leading indicators define the actions necessary to achieve the goal with measurable outcome. They "lead" to meeting overall objectives.

The production schedule allows the crew and cast to do advance planning to meet key milestones. Areas that are often of particular interest are human resources and items dependent on the supply chain.

Once this document is completed, the professional salesperson's role of directing this winning buying experience should be reduced. You are passing the torch to your crew and the new director of the special resource. Successfully passing the torch means providing the crew and director with clear communication and insights. Many projects get off to a slow and clumsy start because this stage was not handled well. The good feeling from a successful sale with a hopeful customer looking to achieve their goals and avoid or get out of the pit of despair can erode quickly if a smooth transition is not made. I recommend once again to slow down before you are engrossed in the next deal.

> *Successfully passing the torch means providing the crew and director with clear communication and insights.*

I'd like to conclude with lessons I have taken away from being in sales for thirty years, training wonderful teams at companies of all sizes, and being fascinated by the movie business. I've tried to give you my top thoughts that also summarize some of the key concepts in this book.

As a fun exercise, I'd love it if you add some more lessons learned from Hollywood that we can share with the Whetstone community. Until then, see you at the movies (after I close my next deal).

# CHAPTER 10

# LESSONS LEARNED FROM HOLLYWOOD

*Dream as if you'll live forever. Live as if you'll die today.*
**—James Dean, actor**

## Lesson One: It All Starts with a Pitch

Some people speculate that the term "elevator pitch" started in Hollywood where an individual would have less than thirty seconds in an elevator to quickly pitch a studio executive on a movie idea. Others attribute the phrase to Elisha Otis, founder of Otis Elevator Company. Otis wanted to create a safe automatic system to move people and debris. At that time elevators were risky because cables would snap, and the elevator would plunge to the bottom of the shaft. He came up with safety locks that would stop a disastrous fall; however, people didn't believe him.

Unable to sell his invention, Otis staged a public demonstration in New York City to prove its efficacy. He stood on top of an elevator car while his assistant cut the cable. Needless to say, the safety locks worked, and sales skyrocketed. Otis Elevator Company still exists today, and we gained the expression "elevator pitch." I like both explanations, although I wouldn't advocate Elisha's demo technique.

We can learn a lot from experts who advise screenwriters on how to pitch a movie. The first thing they recommend is to set a clear pitch goal: the listener must be intrigued enough to receive the screenplay and set up a follow-up meeting. Then create a very short pitch that includes why it's an important story to tell, the genre, plotline summary, existing movie examples, and a call to action. In business speak you're proposing why your solution should be a priority for a company in a specific industry, how you will accomplish it, where it's currently working, and what to do next.

And one more thing about pitches. Hollywood is risk averse. Pitching is getting harder and harder because decision makers believe it's risky to try new ideas. They just keep remaking old movies, sequels, or versions of Broadway plays. Unfortunately, that formula does not always minimize risk. Just look at the movie flop of *Dear Evan Hansen*, which was a phenomenal hit on Broadway.

When salespeople take this risk-averse approach, it's a lot of wash, rinse, and repeat. They don't figure out what the customer needs. They just say, "Hey, we've done this before; let's just keep doing it." And eventually it flops, because it wasn't tailored to what was needed.

## Lesson Two: Movies and Sales Need Engaging and Logical Story Structures

Engaging movies have a logical flow in their plots—a story structure. As I mentioned, stories generally have a beginning, middle, and end (with the middle being the messiest part). Aristotle in 343 BC wanted to find out why stories were so compelling to the human brain and if there was a structure or formula that could be consistently applied. He started studying stories and discovered that there was a common structure that the best stories followed—every story had a crisis, a struggle, and a resolution. Our job as professional salespeople is to help our customers articulate the crisis, get through the struggle, and find a successful resolution. This is the hero's journey.

## Lesson Three: Remember Emotions

Movies work when there's a logical flow throughout the plot as well as emotional touchpoints that move the audience. That's not unlike the sales process. As viewers we may be unhappy when a plot does not follow logic, but we'll totally disengage if we are not feeling emotion. Fear. Joy. Happiness. Sorrow. We need to feel emotionally engaged with the storyline and the hero.

Remember how people make decisions. The truth (which we often forget or deny) is that the logical part of the brain does not make decisions. When we're spouting features and benefits, we're only engaging the logical part of the brain; we make

> *Our job as professional salespeople is to help our customers articulate the crisis, get through the struggle, and find a successful resolution. This is the hero's journey.*

decisions emotionally.[20] That's true in any kind of sale. We need to capture emotions first and then move into the logic used to justify a decision.

---

20   Lisa Cron, *Wired for Story* (Berkeley, CA: Ten Speed Press, 2012).

Marketers often refer to that as the "emotional hook" and the "intellectual alibi." The whole purpose of telling a story is to make somebody feel something. We forget that stories are emotional, so we're trying to sell technically and overlook the emotional impact and significance of the story.

# Lesson Four: Relate to the Hero

In the beginning of a story, the effective storyteller presents a main character. We call that character the hero (Aristotle would have called that character the protagonist). We see the story through the eyes of this hero. For the story to be compelling, the hero has to be relatable to the audience. We need to identify with the hero in a time of crisis. If we relate to the hero in the movie, then we want the hero to win. For the hero to win, they must reach their goal.

Two examples of successful Hollywood stories with relatable heroes are *The Sopranos* and *Breaking Bad*. In *The Sopranos* the main character, Tony Soprano, is a violent mobster who is initially presented in such a way that the audience cares for him. We get to see his vulnerability through his therapy sessions with his psychiatrist. We see how much he cares for his family and the influence of his unreasonable, unfair, and possibly psychopathic mother.

In a similar fashion, Walter White in *Breaking Bad* is presented sympathetically. After cofounding Gray Matter Technologies, he sells his shares at a low price only to find out afterward that the company made a fortune from his research. Soon after, he is diagnosed with lung cancer, and his goal is to secure his family's financial health before he dies. Heroes matter, whether in movies or in a sales setting. Bring them to life, and people will relate on an emotional level.

# Lesson Five: The Villain Drives the Plot

One of the most important takeaway points I would like you to get from this book is that the villain (external forces that put business in a constant state of uncertainty) drives the plot. They are at the center of the hero's journey. Every time the villain puts an obstacle between the hero and their goal, the hero has a decision to make. If the goal isn't that important, the hero gives up, and the story is over. If the goal matters, the hero is going to find a way to overcome the obstacle. Every time the villain puts an obstacle in front of the hero, it causes the hero to make a decision to go over, under, around, or through the obstacle, and that sequence of decisions becomes the plotline of the story.

# Lesson Six: Embrace Empathy

Great movies take it up a notch by creating empathy. You literally feel what's happening to the hero and supporting characters and relate based on your own life experience. I believe that one reason I am successful in professional sales is because I am empathetic. From an early age, I was highly empathetic to the pain and needs of others. This isn't always a strength. I remember years ago when a neighbor was hospitalized due to a very serious ailment. He survived, and months later we were both mowing our lawns. I stopped to talk with him and inquire about his health. I was sorry I did. He went into so much detail I began to feel physically ill. I had to abruptly excuse myself because in a matter of minutes I might have thrown up. After gathering myself I returned to finish the lawn. My neighbor was still out, so he came up to me and said, "As I was saying…" Fortunately, there wasn't much of the story left.

Sometimes I wish I wasn't so empathetic, but it has definitely helped me in sales. When I am creating a positive buying experience, I deeply empathize with the hero and understand them as a unique human being. I win business because the person sitting across from me knows that I understand them and what they're trying to accomplish. They understand that I am committed to helping them accomplish their goals and will get things done in my organization to make sure their needs are met.

People need to feel cared for, especially in our fast-paced, complex business environment. A computer does not make you feel cared for. People need that human-to-human interaction that says, "I can tell Adrian's got my back. He understands me. I can step forward into an unknown future, knowing that I've formed a relationship with somebody that truly cares about me, wants me to be successful, and can pivot and navigate with me."

# Lesson Seven: Understand the Power of Transformation

One of the most successful formulas in moviemaking is the "transformative narrative" where the moviegoer loses themselves in a story and their own attitudes and intentions change. They have been persuaded to see the world in a different way.

One of my customers is involved in almost every aspect the consumer goes through to sell, lease, or buy a car. They realize that many people, particularly the millennial generation, don't want to own a car, and, if they do, they will purchase in a different way. This shift creates a major challenge for my customer and their customers who are made up of major dealer groups.

My customer is shifting to meet the needs of their customers by creating a new transformative narrative that sells the future state. They are helping their customers understand where the automotive industry is heading and how they can be instrumental in creating it. They are selling change—not just a tangible product or service. The company is also changing how it listens to people by shifting from listening as people in the automotive industry to listening with the ears of the channel and the end consumer, and then aligning multiple perspectives around a win-win-win initiative. This allows them to nuance their communications to be aligned with internal and external stakeholders and shape the many changes we are beginning to see in the automotive industry. That's the power of transformation.

As sales professionals who are creating transformative narratives, we need to follow what Dr. Tony Alessandra calls "the platinum rule." The platinum rule represents the true theological interpretation of the golden rule: "Do unto others as you would have them to do unto you." The platinum rule says think about what the customer wants and do that instead of thinking and doing what you want. Or as articulated by Zig Ziglar, "You can get everything in life you want if you will just help enough other people get what they want." It's vital that this philosophy of serving others filters down all levels of the sales process, because the world has changed and continues to change rapidly.

# Lesson Eight: The Audience Is Smart

Moviegoers, and particularly fans, are smart. They know when a plot doesn't make sense. They scrutinize dialogue, costumes, and dialects for inconsistency. They are whistleblowers on illogical diversions in a storyline or character portrayal, particularly in movie franchises like

Marvel or *Star Wars*. And with social media, moviegoers can easily kill a movie's success, even if the critics love it. Just look at Rotten Tomatoes' dual-rating system that shares scores from critics *and* the public to see the power of moviegoers.

The world of sales is not much different. Today, customers have so much information through the internet that they may know more about the item or service they are interested in purchasing than the sales professional who is selling it. They also are not shy about voicing opinions. Additionally, it's increasingly difficult to get in front of people. They don't want to meet with salespeople. They prefer to do analysis and research on their own, and then make their decision.

It used to be simple: put the products in the trunk of your car, drive around, take the catalog, do some demonstrations, and people would figure out if the product would work for them. Until recently sales were often based on relationships and the affinity the salesperson and customer felt for each other. That's what I talked about in *Human to Human Selling* ten years ago. Salespeople with good personalities were able to build trust and friendship; a lot of sales happened that way.

We've seen that diminish over time. Now, we're entering into environments that are more complex and, equally important, constantly changing. Companies are shifting their emphasis from relationship selling to consultative selling, which means asking questions in order to understand and demonstrate the solution. Additionally, our customers need to buy a solution that's somewhat future proof, can handle increasing complexity, and can adapt to a changing environment.

If you're going to successfully sell your solution into a constantly changing environment, you need to come into that environment and understand what's going on, who's who, and what the objectives are. You need to proactively work to understand how the environment is changing. What was installed three months ago may require tweaking based on what you're seeing today. This ability to anticipate change in order to ensure an ongoing fit requires a smarter and more empathetic approach to selling.

## Lesson Nine: There Are a Lot of Players Involved

While I've been focusing on the hero in movies, there are a lot of other people involved: the supporting actors, the crew, the director, the producer, and so on. Obviously, just a few are involved in the actual final decision-making about the film, but many share in the success of the movie. That's the same in professional sales.

Let's focus on the decision makers in companies. More and more stakeholders are getting involved in decision-making. Twenty years ago there would be two key stakeholders deciding; ten years ago the number was seven. Now, there are more than a dozen key stakeholders. With more complexity nobody wants to just take a chance without getting full buy-in from everybody else. Often, salespeople miss this dynamic.

## Lesson Ten: Storyboards Are a Great Tool

Storyboards are graphic organizers that plan narratives. Filmmakers use storyboards to save time and money as well as build consensus among a team. This tool is used before any movie is shot to capture key information in a sequenced and practical way and is referred to often to make sure things are on track or need to be adjusted. Storyboarding is particularly useful when directors are less experienced or working in a new genre, because it provides discipline, clarity, structure, and answers to important questions before the crew is engaged. Can this tool be adapted for professional sales? Absolutely.

## Lesson Eleven: Sequels Are Profitable

Hollywood loves its sequels. That's because they make money. In a 2016 analysis by *Forbes,* the publication found that fifteen of the top twenty most profitable movies were sequels, spin-offs, or reboots.[21]

The same is true in professional sales. It's easier to sell to your fans (existing customers), because they know and like you. Additionally, getting the original sale often takes investment of time and money that can be recouped in subsequent sales. Long-term customers are the foundation of any successful company.

The caution, of course, is not to become complacent. Many service companies have suffered debilitating revenue losses when a long-term customer leaves, and they have an empty pipeline. Additionally, complacency can lead to not doing proper discovery. Every sale is new, and if you make assumptions, particularly in areas like the villain and the flaw, you may not be doing a sequel.

## Lesson Twelve: Success Depends On a Good Director

The category of Best Director is one of the most competitive in the Academy Awards. It generally goes to directors who make a movie

---

21   Katie Sola, "Want to Produce a Profitable Movie? Make a Sequel," Forbes. com, February 15, 2016, https://www.forbes.com/sites/katiesola/2016/02/25/ want-to-produce-a-profitable-movie-make-a-sequel/.

that is both an artistic and commercial win. Even more impressive is when accomplished actors like Salma Hayek praise a director, in this case Angelina Jolie for *Without Blood:* "I was completely blown away by her mind, her dedication, her technical knowledge, and her control of every aspect, as well as her vision which is so clear. She is so good with the actors, so passionate, and so focused. But most of all, I was blown away by her kindness to every single person on the set."[22]

When they are operating at the top of their game, professional salespeople and strategic account managers also have that kind of impact and earn that kind of respect from prospects and customers. Moreover, they treat their crew with the utmost respect, which motivates everyone going the extra mile to ensure important customer outcomes are achieved.

# Conclusion

Congratulations! You've made it to the end. Well, it's the end of the book but, hopefully, the beginning of a fresh approach to sales or strategic account management for you. The concept is simple but profound. You're not the hero in the movie—your customer is. Your role and your real value is to be the special resource. To be valued as the special resource, you must help your customer understand the full context of their situation. That context starts with their important goals—professional and personal.

Once the goals are understood, the next most important thing is to help them understand how the world is changing around them in ways that are adversarial and out of their control. This loss of control

---

22    Rosy Cordero, "Salma Hayek Pinault Praises 'Genius' Angelina Jolie's Directing Skills in 'Without Blood'; Talks Empowering Women with New Eva Perón Series," Deadline.com, August 18, 2022, https://deadline.com/2022/08/salma-hayek-pinault-angelina-jolie-without-blood-santa-evita-1235088340/.

creates a sense of urgency, but fighting against external forces outside of one's control is pointless. If they do nothing, they will be overwhelmed by these external forces and will lose everything in the pit of despair.

While these forces are out of their control, it doesn't mean they are completely helpless and destined for despair. They aren't helpless, because they can change. They can become stronger, faster, or smarter in order to successfully adapt to their new situation. And that's where you come in as the special resource.

The value of the special resource is to provide the hero with new and relevant capabilities and competencies that they are unable to acquire by themselves. To be a truly special resource, you must think beyond your standard products and/or services and configure solutions that are highly relevant to the customer's situation and highly differentiated from any other solution available to them.

As a result of your special resource, they can emerge from or completely avoid the pit of despair. They can enter the new world as a victor. What is most important about their journey is not just the fact that they've won; it's the fact that the journey has transformed them. They can look back with a sense of gratitude for the setback because of their transformation (i.e., what they've become in the process).

And as you go from customer to customer and project to project, you can look back with a great sense of fulfillment. Not just because of your new level of success, but more importantly because of your legacy. You will be among those rare people who make the world a better place by making others better. As we rapidly advance into a brave new world filled with robots,

*You will be among those rare people who make the world a better place by making others better.*

automation, and artificial intelligence, people are craving genuine human connection.

I leave you with a quotation that impacted me when I started my journey in sales and that remains top of mind:

> *"You can get everything you want in life if you will help enough other people to get what they want."*
> **—Zig Ziglar**

May you use your special powers to help enough other people get what they want!

## ABOUT THE AUTHOR

**A**drian Davis is the president and CEO of Whetstone Inc., a management consulting firm. Companies such as 3M, Merck, Owens Illinois, Johnson & Johnson, AVI-SPL, Cox Automotive, bioMerieux, and John Deere have worked with Adrian to create greater value for their customers. He is a certified speaking professional (CSP), a certified professional in business process management (P.BPM), and a certified competitive intelligence professional (CIP).

The author of *Heroes, Villains, and the Thrill of Professional Selling* and *Human to Human Selling,* Adrian is an internationally recognized, thought-provoking speaker and trusted advisor to CEOs and sales leaders. He uses his advanced skills in storytelling and his deep insight into the sales and buying process to inspire salespeople to reach higher levels of performance. He is frequently called upon to address executive teams and sales groups on the subjects of selling value and sales excellence as he discusses sales as a valuable service.

# GET IN TOUCH

Thank you for your interest in reaching out to Adrian Davis, the author of *Heroes, Villains, and the Thrill of Professional Selling*. We would be happy to help with any inquiries or questions you may have about the book or about Adrian's keynote speeches and training workshops.

Adrian can be reached at info@whetsoneinc.ca, and you can also contact him at 877-947-9047.

For more information on Adrian's approach to selling, visit his online learning platform, The Whetstone Institute of Sales Transformation, at twist.whetstoneinc.ca.

Adrian is available for keynote speeches and training workshops on strategic selling and strategic account management. His presentations are tailored to the specific needs of each organization, and he has experience working with businesses of all sizes and industries.

You can also connect with Adrian on LinkedIn (https://www.linkedin.com/in/adriandavis/) and Twitter (@theAdrianDavis), where he frequently shares insights and updates on the latest trends and strategies in professional selling.

Thank you for considering Adrian as a speaker or trainer for your organization. We look forward to hearing from you soon.

Printed in the USA
CPSIA information can be obtained
at www.ICGtesting.com
JSHW021623280823
47399JS00001B/7

9 781642 255461